Shattered Innocence

KELLY VATES

Evergreen
PRESS

Shattered Innocence
by Kelly Vates

ISBN 1-58169-066-5
For Worldwide Distribution
Printed in the U.S.A.

Evergreen Press
P.O. Box 91011 • Mobile, AL 36691
800-367-8203

Publisher's note: Some of the names of people in this book have been changed to protect their privacy.

The photographs in this book are of professional models who have no connection with the story or the problem of abuse.

TABLE OF CONTENTS

ACKNOWLEDGMENTS

I would like to express my deepest gratitude to the many people who supported me and the ministry of this book. To my faithful brothers and sisters of The First Christian Church of Hessville, the words "thank you" are just not enough. Your constant prayers and unconditional support mean the world to me. May God bless you all.

To my father, Thomas Daniel, who showed me the path of recovery. Because you believed in me, I dared to believe in myself. I thank God for the relationship we have today.

To my Monday night therapy group: thank you, my friends and fellow survivors for a safe place to heal. This book honors you!

To my children, Erika, Jeremy, and Emily: thank you for teaching me the meaning of true joy. The laughter I have shared with you has been the greatest healing of all. I thank God each day for choosing me to be your mom.

To my husband and friend, Joseph: thank you for persevering, for believing in us when I didn't, for taking care of me when I couldn't care for myself. Most of all, thank you for leading our family in the faith. I love you more each day.

Thank you, Evergreen Press, for having the courage and the faith to publish this book. God truly brought us together.

My final words of gratitude I offer to my heavenly Father. I thank you, Father, for your guidance in my life. Thank you for never turning from me even when I turned from you. Thank you for crying with me during the abuse because You were hurting, too. Thank you for carrying me through the blackest days when death was all I longed for. Thank you for your patience as I walked my recovery path. Most of all, Father, thank you for restoring my soul! My prayer is that Thy will be done in my life and with this book.

DEDICATION

This book is dedicated to every survivor
of childhood sexual abuse,
in remembrance of the pain you endured
and in honor of your courage
as you walk the path of recovery.
May God bless you
and keep you and give you peace.

INTRODUCTION

Childhood should be a time of innocence and wonder...a time full of jump rope, hop scotch, and baseball...a time when you spend those magical moments just before dark trying to catch fireflies. It's in these times, in these moments, that innocence can be shattered, and a child's love can be twisted and manipulated into something dirty and shameful. After each sexual abuse encounter, the little girl is left alone to carry on as though nothing has happened. Burdened with terrible secrets they have been threatened to keep, these girls grow up looking for Prince Charming and praying for "happily ever after" to begin.

As a survivor of childhood sexual abuse, this was how I lived. I learned years ago to wear a permanent mask for the outside world to see, and after I was married and had children, I continued to put it on. From the outside, the world saw a wonderful family. I am a stay-at-home mom with a loving husband and three beautiful children. Our lives are full of school and soccer games and trips to the park. However, when the doors were shut and the blinds were closed, I ate and drank to numb my pain. I was dying inside, choking on the pain of the past. I even prayed to die. Life as I knew it was nothing but pain. This was about to begin to change....Welcome to my story, my name is Kelly.

*The story of Cinderella is really
the tale of an abused and neglected child.
Her story is my story but without the
dramatic rescue. Thankfully, someone
finally showed me the way to a healthy life.*

CHAPTER ONE

Happily Ever After

The story of Cinderella is really the tale of an abused and neglected child who was eventually rescued from dreadful circumstances. As we all know, she married Prince Charming and was whisked away to enjoy a life filled with "happily-ever-after."

Her story is also my story but without the dramatic rescue. My story includes not just physical abuse and neglect, but also childhood sexual abuse, rape, and abortion. For many long years, castles seemed far away from my simple Indiana home, and happy endings weren't on the horizon. Thankfully, someone better than a fairy godmother eventually showed me the way, and my story became transformed into one of hope, healing, and recovery.

Welcome to my story. It began once upon a time when my real father was sent to Viet Nam in the late 60s without even knowing I was on the way. My parents' marriage was troubled from the very beginning, and they divorced as soon as he returned. Not long afterward, my stepfather entered the story and created havoc in our lives. Compared to what I endured, Cinderella had it easy. If all I ever had to do was work hard and suffer the taunts of wicked stepsisters, it probably wouldn't have taken so many years to heal from the emotional scars I received.

Cinderella never had to live through my nightmare. My stepfather physically abused my mom and brother; and before I was even old enough to attend school, he began to sexually abuse me. He was a man who worshiped Elvis Presley and thought he looked just like him, sideburns and all. He had a strong jawbone that gave him a fierce, dominating look.

When I was a young child, my stepfather led me to believe that sex was love. "Show Daddy how much you love him," he'd say as he guided my hand in the direction that he desired. He took my innocent love and desire to be loved and twisted them into something horrible, filling me with shame. He used me but never loved me. After one episode of oral sex, I began to gag and didn't make it to the bathroom in time. I vomited in the hallway, causing him to whip me and throw me into my own vomit. I was only five years old at the time.

Each time my stepfather forced himself on me, I begged God to send my real daddy home to save me. I promised God that I would be a good girl and never ask for anything else again if He would just send my daddy home, but He never did. It wasn't until a long time later that I understood why. Thankfully, my stepfather was sent to prison for trying to rob a bank and imprisoned for a few years.

When he was released on parole, I was frightened the abuse would start all over again, so I told my Grandma, who was devastated by the news. When my mother was informed, she dragged me to my stepfather's apartment and confronted him. Of course, he never admitted to it and threatened to whip me for lying. After we left his place, my mother coldly dropped me off at dance class and picked me up two hours later. She never talked with me about the abuse...not then, not ever. That was our family's way—if you didn't talk about something, it ceased to exist.

That wasn't the end of the abuse I endured. When another person began to abuse me before I was even in high school, I was convinced that it was all my fault. Somehow, I believed I deserved it. I believed I was worthless. I began to hate myself and pray that I would die because that seemed like the only way out. As the years went by, I began to think that my connection to God's answering service had been disconnected.

Prince Charming

So, what was left for a Cinderella with no fairy godmother? According to the fairy tale, I was supposed to find a young prince, fall in love (even though I had no idea what real love was), and live happily ever after. In other words, I needed someone who would care for me and take me away from all the pain. The prospect of living "happily ever after" sounded wonderful.

I will be the first to admit that I entered into marriage for all the wrong reasons. For that, I am sorry. However, I am *not sorry* for marrying Joe. Even though I doubted that God was listening to my prayers, in later years I could see how He was always there beside me. When God sent Joe into my life, He gave me a wonderful gift.

Joe has soft, wavy brown hair and freckles on his face and arms. He looks so much like the "boy next door" that people told me I was marrying Opie! Joe's most endearing quality is his incredible sense of humor. Joe laughs all day long because he has the gift of finding joy in life's smallest things. He's a shining light in the darkness for me. They say you're attracted to the person who has the characteristics that you wish to possess. That's true for me—Joe's deep reservoir of joy was something I wanted to drink deeply from; I wanted happiness the way he had it. So I married my prince. Happily ever after was supposed to begin.

I stood in the shower on my wedding day and said to myself, "My life begins today. I can forget everything that has ever happened to me up until this point." The problem with fairy tales is that the authors never tell you how to get over the hurts and scars of the previous 20 years so that you *can* live happily. Even my wonderful Joe could not transform my life as much as he wanted to.

Within a short period of time, I concluded that happily ever after was not possible. I had thought that all the pain was going to miraculously disappear after we got married. Isn't that what happened to Cinderella? Where was the happiness I desperately wanted? Drawing the life out of my husband didn't give me the deep sense of peace and joy that I longed for.

If getting married wasn't the answer, then what was? How do people find true joy and happiness? What would it take to make me happy? What would stop the aching pain deep within my soul?

My answer to these questions was that Cinderella needed to have a baby. Again, I will be the first one to admit that I got pregnant for all the wrong reasons, but I will *never* say that I'm sorry for having my baby. When I felt life inside me, it was the first form of true joy I ever experienced. My baby…my child…my joy! It was as if I lived because she lived. It wasn't the right answer, but it was the place where my path toward wholeness first began.

I became the mother of the most beautiful, black haired, 7lb. 12oz. baby girl I had ever seen—my precious Erika. She was everything I wasn't. I felt that I had finally become special because I was her mother. During the first middle-of-the-night feeding, I held my sweet little baby and promised her, "I don't know why God gave you to me. I don't deserve to be your mommy, but I will do everything in my power to make sure you always know how loved and special you are." She slept peacefully the rest of the night.

Reality Sets In

Reality can be a brutal thing. I came home from the hospital that hot August day with my beautiful baby and thought that finally my life was getting better. But I had no idea how much work was ahead—the sleepless nights, the endless diaper changes, the monotonous rocking for hours, the batch after batch of formula that had to be mixed. I was surprised that caring for a baby could make a person feel so exhausted.

After we brought her home, Joe helped me with everything because I felt so overwhelmed with the responsibilities of motherhood. He was so natural at being a good father. When Erika began screaming right after her birth, Joe whispered, "Erika, don't cry. Daddy's here," and she immediately hushed. While she was still in the womb, he had read to her almost every night, and she evidently recognized his voice. He's a great father, and I depended so much on him.

The next month, my burdens multiplied. Joe worked as a manager for a large toy store. Because the Christmas retail season begins in September and extends through February, Joe now had to be at the store for 12 and sometimes 14 hours a day. Suddenly I was home alone with my baby most of the time. Not only did I experience lack of sleep and increased responsibilities, now I also missed the one person who could bring a smile to my face.

Unaware of what was happening, I quickly slipped into a depression. I stayed in bed as much as I could. When Erika napped, I napped. When Erika ate, I ate—and that was often. Whatever I could find, I ate. Stuffing myself with food was the only way I could seem to fill the emptiness inside. It didn't matter what food I ate, I just felt better when I did. I used food like novocaine to stop the pain, but it only had a temporary effect. From time to time I also drank alcohol, but I couldn't afford much. I ached with loneliness. Joe was my prince, but nowhere in the story does it say that Cinderella was left at the castle all alone with a baby that needed constant attention. My fairy tale dreams deceived me.

I told myself to hang on because soon things would get better. But less than four months later, I became pregnant again. What a surprise! (I say *surprise* because a *mistake* is something you receive but would change if you could. On the other hand, a surprise is something you unexpectedly receive but wouldn't change for the world.) In September, our wonderful, fuzzy haired son Jeremy was born.

This was a frightening time for me. I knew in my heart that I had no idea how to love a boy. Thankfully he was an easy baby to care for—he slept much more than Erika ever did—but why did God give me a son? I understood Erika's needs because I once was a little girl with the same needs, but I had absolutely no idea what a little boy needed. I was scared and overwhelmed, so I pulled away from everyone and sank deeper into my depression. I had nightmares and panic attacks in the middle of the night and very rarely got dressed unless I knew someone was coming over or I had to go somewhere. I ate everything and anything and drank alcohol whenever I could. I was spinning out of control.

Depression Takes Over

From time to time, I tried shaking loose from my despondency. I found a part-time job, but that didn't last long. Minimum wage is barely make enough to pay for the sitter and gas. For awhile I watched the young boy from downstairs after school, but a third child in the home only caused me to feel more overwhelmed. So we moved across town because we thought that a change of scenery might help me. We found a very old white house for rent with huge shrubs and pine trees in front that needed a lot of fixing up,. Keeping busy was good for me because it helped me ignore the pain. But after all the painting and redecorating and unpacking was over with, I was left alone again with all my pain. We were more secluded than ever before since on one side of our house was an open field that belonged to our only neighbor—the perfect setting for someone who wanted nothing to do with the world. I could sit outside while the kids played, wearing the same clothes for days, and no one would know the difference. Now I was depressed *and* isolated.

During this time, I attended church regularly. I heard lots of Bible teaching, but had no idea how to apply it to my life. I no longer believed that God could take away my pain. Even though I spent time with the people from church, I had no clue how to get the inner peace they had. Joe was the only one who saw me for all that I was and, amazingly, still loved me. He tried to make me happy, but he couldn't. No one could. So Joe and I grew farther and farther apart. I tried to be a good mother—I loved my kids, and I put every ounce of energy into them. I read every book and magazine on parenting that I could get my hands on. I spent time with people that

I admired as parents and learned from them.

Even though our marriage had problems, we decided to have another baby. After having difficult deliveries the first two times, we concluded we would only have one more child. We didn't want our children too far apart, so after Jeremy's second birthday we tried to conceive. In some respects, I think we were trying to bring ourselves closer together since we always felt closer when I was pregnant. The following September, in the midst of my depression, I delivered Emily, our little ray of sunshine.

During these first five years of marriage, I desperately tried to numb my feelings with food and alcohol. By the time Emily was six months old, I weighed more than 300 pounds and had to fight myself not to take a drink before noon. I hid my drinking problem from everyone—even Joe—but my overeating was probably obvious to anyone who saw me. I was ashamed. I was ashamed of the way I looked. I was ashamed of the way I felt inside. I was especially ashamed of myself because I had three beautiful children and a loving husband but no idea how to appreciate them. I didn't understand how to allow myself to feel joy inside. I called myself a Christian, attended church on Sundays, and said all the things I was taught to say, but I had no idea how to live a healthy, normal life. I lost faith in God and in myself. I lost the will to live. I had hit bottom.

CHAPTER TWO

And the Rain Came

The bottom is a very difficult place to be. When you're in the middle of a depression, it's hard to discern the difference between *fact* and *feeling*. I *felt* alone and isolated. The *fact* of the matter is that I wasn't alone. I had my loving husband and three wonderful children with me every day. I had childhood friends who were just a phone call away. Joe's family lived nearby, and we spent lots of time with them. We discussed the kids, T.V. shows, sports, and everyday family problems, although I never shared my pain with any of them. I also had friends at church that I visited occasionally. They, too, had no idea what I was going through.

I felt completely alone, trapped in the pain from my past, with no means of escape to a happy future. I didn't believe that anyone could understand my hurt. I convinced myself that these lies were the truth. I couldn't see or feel anything but pain; nothing I did seemed to help. I tried to stuff the pain down into the dark recesses of my memory, but I began to have panic attacks again. I pretended that the sexual abuse never happened, but that didn't work either—it only caused more flashbacks and nightmares. I tried to forget, but my mind wouldn't let me. I used alcohol to numb the pain, but it only relieved the pain for a short time and returned worse than ever. Pain always gave me a hollow feeling inside, so I stuffed it with food, but it only made me gain more weight, which depressed me all the more. I even tried prayer. I prayed from my mouth and my head the things that I memorized as a child, but it just made me feel abandoned by God and more alone. In my opinion, "happily ever after" was a lie, and I wanted out of the story. I finally decided to put a stop to the pain by ending my life. I had already ceased living emotionally a long time before.

When I began to consider my options for suicide, I refused to bring pain to my three wonderful children. I decided to find a way to make my death look like an accident to protect them, and that spring, I began to plan my death in earnest. I thought about driving the car off an expressway ramp, but there was no guarantee of death in such an "accident." I thought about blowing out the pilot light on the stove, but I was never home alone. I even thought about taking an overdose, but I had no idea what kind of drugs to use or where to get them. I felt frustrated. Was I so incapable that I couldn't even figure out how to kill myself?

Then one cool evening in mid April, Emily woke up during the night, which was not normal for her since she didn't have nighttime feedings any more. Pulling a robe around my nightgown, I climbed the stairs to see what was wrong. By the time I made it to her room, she had stopped crying and was already back to sleep. *Bad dream,* I thought, as I stood over her crib and looked in wonderment at my precious child. I touched her angelic face softly as tears ran down my face.

On my way down the hall, I stopped in Erika's and Jeremy's rooms. I watched them both sleep in such peace. How I longed for that same peace! It came so naturally for them. I realized then that no matter how I took my life, it would cause them pain. I have moved heaven and earth in order for my children not to experience pain, so I decided that I didn't want to cause them the worst pain they would ever experience in their lives.

Angry With God

That instant, I went from being sad to being extremely angry. There was only one person to talk with at three in the morning and that was God. I went downstairs where no one could hear me and spent the next two and a half hours screaming at Him. I blamed God for not preventing my stepfather from hurting me. I berated Him because He never sent my real daddy home to save me. I screamed at Him for never hearing my prayers and never stopping the pain. I continued to shout accusations at Him, and then I began to cry. I cried for the little girl that was hurt so badly and who still hurt today. I cried for all my lost hopes and dreams. I cried for my children because I felt they deserved a better mother. I cried for my husband because he loved me, and I had no idea how to love him. I cried until I couldn't cry any more...until there was nothing coming out but whimpers that sounded more like a child than an adult woman.

My anger was finally spent; I was exhausted. Suddenly I could smell the rain through the screened window. It was sprinkling gently outside, and lightning in the distance made the room glow softly every now and then. I sat quietly in my chair watching the water drip off the roof when slowly I began to feel warmth surround me. Suddenly I knew God had heard me. For the first time in my life, I had prayed from my heart and not my mouth. For the first time, my heart cried out to God for help, and I gave up trying to fix it myself—I had tried and failed miserably. Before I finally went back to bed, I looked out the window and watched the sun begin to come up. I said, "God, I'll give You one last chance."

Learning to Trust

When I awoke from my short sleep that morning, I was scared. I didn't really know how to trust God. In my mind, trust was something *earned* not given. My experience with trusting my stepfather had horrible results. Because of that, even my heavenly Father had to earn my trust. In the beginning, I allowed Him only a small part of my heart. If He proved trustworthy, I might give Him a little more. I was scared, but I was out of options. Where should I begin?

God knew me pretty well, and He knew I needed some fast evidence of His help. I needed to see with my own eyes some tangible evidence of His love and concern for me. I focused on my weight. It made me feel bad about myself, but it was something that provided a difference I could actually measure. I began a weight program that included videos and a recommended diet.

In less than six months, I lost almost 70 pounds! I thought that from here on out, things were only going to get better because God was really working in my life. During this time, my husband went to a Promise Keepers convention and had a spiritual awakening himself. It was there that Joe made a decision to stop drinking altogether. I told him that if he would quit, so would I. Believe it or not, it was easy for me to quit. I will admit that my weight loss slowed down because I was eating more to compensate, but I felt pretty good about things.

Could this be the beginning of happily ever after? Actually, it was God giving me some growing room because He had a larger plan. I couldn't see it, but it had been unfolding behind the scenes for quite some time. He blessed me with the weight loss to give me some self-confidence. I needed it for what lie ahead; I also needed to be sober. God was in control now. You've probably heard the saying, "Be careful what you pray for." Well, it's true. Fasten your seatbelts, because when you pray from the heart, that's when the ride really begins!

CHAPTER THREE

Back to the Beginning

When God began to restore me, He started from the beginning of my life. The many prayers I had said asking Him to send my daddy back home were finally going to be answered!

I had tried to find my father once when I was about 12 years old. My stepfather was gone by then, and my mother, two brothers, two sisters, and I lived in a small two-bedroom ranchhouse that belonged to my grandmother. My Grandma took care of us while my mother worked to put food on the table. Grandma always seemed beautiful to me. She looked like a typical grandmother in those days with creamy skin that hardly ever saw any makeup and black hair that was always permed. Grandma was what we used to proudly call "pleasingly plump" so that when I hugged her, she felt soft.

Uncle Henry

Because she never learned to drive, Grandma often walked to her brother's house about four blocks from ours. One afternoon, on her way home, she ran into one of my dad's brothers named Henry. Grandma rushed home and told me about her encounter with my uncle. She wanted me to go right away and introduce myself, but I really didn't want to go—I was afraid to find out the truth. Grandma, however, was not the kind of person who took no for an answer. She looked me square in the eye and said, "Kelly, this is your chance. If you want to know anything about your father, you better get over there."

I dragged my feet the entire way to Uncle Henry's house. I was only 12 years old and shook inside with much more than the normal insecurity of that age. I stood all alone at their door and wasn't even sure if I was knocking on the right one. When a petite, attractive woman answered, I couldn't say anything but, "I'm Kelly."

The lady smiled warmly at me and invited me inside. She had evidently been expecting me. Introducing herself as Laura, she gently guided me to the kitchen where two men were sitting at the table. Pointing to the smaller man, she said, "This is Henry." Then a small girl, about five years old, with light brown hair named Mary skipped into the kitchen. I remember looking at her and thinking to myself that she looked quite a bit like me at that age.

Henry ignored me at first and continued his conversation with the other man while I sat stiffly on the hard kitchen chair, waiting my turn. Finally Henry turned his attention to me and asked me a question. I don't remember what it was. Henry made me nervous, and it was all I could do to blurt out, "Where's my dad?" That's all I wanted to know.

Henry didn't seem to be comfortable talking to me either. He shifted in his chair and said, "I don't know, the last I heard, he was in southern Indiana working in law enforcement." I got the impression that he didn't want to tell me anything whatsoever about his brother. He finally said he wasn't sure if my dad was still in Indiana or not. Then he delivered the final blow. He said that it had been years since he had heard from him, and my dad still owed Henry money.

I sat there feeling crushed. My heart ached, and I had to force back the tears. Henry returned to his conversation with the other man and seemed to reject me as if it were somehow my fault that my dad skipped town without repaying him the money he had borrowed. I sat there feeling abandoned and scared, not knowing what to do. Mary came back into the kitchen with her favorite game and asked me if I would play with her. I forced a smile at her and said, "Sure." After two games, I thanked her for playing with me and stood up to leave. Mary's little face revealed her disappointment that the fun was over, and she asked me when I was coming back. Sensing how I felt, Laura tried to comfort me with a smile and said that I was always welcome. I lied to Mary that I'd be back the next week and left as quickly as I could.

On the way home, I tried to come to terms with reality. Tears started streaming down my cheeks. For years, all my hopes and prayers were wasted on a man who still owed his brother money. I could hear what Henry was trying to tell me—my father was a good-for-nothing bum. I walked home that day and told myself that if my father was good for nothing, then that must make me at least half good-for-nothing. All those years I wanted to find my father so I could find my identity. What I found was what I had believed all along—that I was worthless. My mind put all of this together in seconds, and I immediately believed it. Why not? The abuse made me feel worthless, and now I had proof that it was true.

I also had to face my shattered dreams—my father was never coming back. No matter how hard I prayed or hoped or wished, it was not going to happen. When I got to our front porch, I wiped the tears away with my sleeve before I went in. I quickly ran to hide myself in the bathroom while I tried to face these ugly truths. Grandma knocked on the door right away.

"How did things go at your Uncle Henry's?" she asked.

I managed to say, "Just fine," but Grandma knew better. She opened the door and saw me standing there with tears running down my face.

"What happened?" she asked.

I told her the awful details, blew my nose, and tried to go to my room. I wanted to be alone so I could take my hurt out and examine it all by myself. But bless her, Grandma wouldn't let me. She hugged me—not just a small hug that you get when you're saying hello to someone. No, not this time. She didn't have any answers to fix my situation; she didn't know what to say to make me feel better. She just gave me a long, warm hug that reached deep down inside of me. She knew my pain ran very deep, and so she held me, slowly rocking me from side to side. She didn't let go until I had stopped crying.

I blew my nose, and she smiled and asked, "Can you make us some cornbread? I'm hungry." I spent the rest of that afternoon on our small cement porch with my Grandma, eating cornbread and talking about, well…really nothing.

Answered Prayer

This incident from childhood seemed like a lifetime ago. But after my middle-of-the-night encounter with God, I kept feeling the urge to make one last attempt to contact my father. Should I dare try to find him? Would it just make everything worse or would it begin to resolve the issues of the past?

I debated over what action to take for days. Finally, I talked with Joe, and he suggested, "Why not try to make contact once again with your Uncle Henry to see if he knows where your father lives? Maybe Henry's listed in the phonebook."

Could it be that easy? Well, surprisingly it was. Checking in the phonebook, I found that my uncle ironically lived just a few blocks away from us. I was amazed that the answers I had longed to receive could be just around the corner. My uncle answered the phone, and I identified myself and explained that I was looking for my father. To my surprise, Uncle Henry said he did know how to contact my father. I asked for a number where I could reach him, and Uncle Henry suggested that he call my dad and give him my number instead. I gave him my phone number and then there was nothing to do but wait. *That was way too easy*, I thought. *Probably nothing will come of this.*

Five days later, I heard my father's voice for the first time! I had been waiting so long to hear the words, "This is your father." My stomach was in knots. All I could reply was a timid, "Hi." I began to panic; I hadn't planned on him calling me. I really believed that he never wanted anything to do with me when I was born, and that he probably felt the same today. I told him I had no idea where to begin. His voice was calm and gentle, and he asked if he could begin. We talked for over two hours about everything that had been on my heart all those years. His voice sounded very caring. No matter how harsh my question, his response was always gentle.

"Why did you leave and never come back? Why did you never check up on me?" I threw question after question at him.

Not once did he give me just a "yes" or a "no" answer. He never evaded my questions, even if they made him uncomfortable. His tone was comforting, and I felt as though I could ask him anything, and so I did.

I told him about my stepfather and the abuse. I told him all the horrid details because I still hurt deeply, and I wanted him to hurt, too. We talked and talked until I knew that, for now, it was time to say goodbye even though I wished we didn't have to end the conversation. I wanted to imprint the sound of his voice in my memory because I was afraid I'd never hear it again. His gentle voice assured me that tonight was only the beginning. He said he would love to be a part of my life, if I would allow him to be. He promised, the only promise he ever has made to me, that I would hear his voice again. He gave me his address and phone number and suggested we send pictures and begin to build a relationship.

Before we hung up, he said the words I had longed to hear all of my life: "Kelly, the reason that I left was not because I didn't love you. I do; I love you very much." My heart broke wide open. I closed my eyes to try to hold back the tears, but there was no keeping them in. My body began to shake with the sobs, and at first the silence from the phone scared me. But then I realized he was crying, too. I responded truthfully from my heart, "I have loved you for a long time." After reassuring me that he would call again the next day, we hung up. I may not have understood all his reasons for never contacting me, but I did know that he loved me now and that was enough for me.

I went to the living room and sat down on the sofa next to my husband. He wrapped his loving arms around me, and I sobbed, "It wasn't my fault!"

CHAPTER FOUR

The Healing Begins

The healing process began in a way that only God could do. My father *did* call back the next day and together we started down a road of discovery. My father shared a lot of things with me, but the one thing he spoke about the most was his own recovery.

God's timing is really wonderful. My father shared that he was a recovering drug addict and had been "clean" for five years when we initially made contact. He understood recovery first hand and knew that I needed to walk down some of the same roads that he had walked. I, on the other hand, had no idea there was such a thing as recovery from sexual abuse. I thought recovery was only for people with drug or alcohol problems. I quit drinking all by myself so I didn't think I needed any help. As for the pain I always carried with me, that's just a part of life, or so I thought at the time.

The Meeting

My dad and I met face to face for the first time two days before my 26th birthday at the airport. I wanted it to be just the two of us and no one else. I was nervous because I so desperately wanted him to like me. I wanted to be *accepted* by him. Even more than accepted, I wanted to be *cherished* by my father. I wanted him to look at me with the same love and pride in his eyes as my husband has when he looks at our daughters. I wanted him to love me unconditionally. I wanted to feel as if I belonged to him. I wanted to feel like his daughter.

When I saw him coming down the ramp, I couldn't believe it was really happening. Here was this average looking man with black hair and dark eyes striding with open arms toward me. The first thing I noticed was his eyes. They were filled with love and compassion and more tenderness than I could have ever hoped for. His embrace was strong but gentle. He told me I was beautiful; and, even though I didn't believe it, I was glad he said it. We left the airport and drove to my home.

I was so excited for him to meet my husband and children. My dad is an easy person to talk to, so Joe and the kids reacted well to him. The kids were too small at the time to fully comprehend who he was, but they enjoyed him all the same. However, I really wanted him all to myself because I had waited so long for this moment. I wanted to shut my regular life off during those four days and just be his daughter. We spent time getting to know each other, and doing a lot together. He spoke at our church and shared his pain and how God took that pain from him. We attended a 12-step meeting together. He came to my birthday party—what a celebration for me that was!

He took me to dinner for my birthday where we exchanged presents since his birthday was just seven days before mine. I bought him a music box that played the song "Daddy's Little Girl." On the top of the box it reads: "It's not the things you do for me that make me love you so, it's the person that you try to be and the friend I've come to know." I also bought him a lighter with "Dad" engraved on it. That was the first time I ever bought something etched with the word "Dad." My father's present to me was a gold cross on a chain with a shroud draped over it. It was the first birthday present my dad ever bought me. I put the cross around my neck and rarely take it off, even to this day. It would take me awhile before I could see how profound this gift was and understand what my father was trying to say.

Dad wanted to go to his mother's gravesite to pay his respects, so I went with him. As we stood by the grave together, I could tell how his heart was aching. I went back to the car to give him some time alone. When he returned from the grave, he was crying. He hugged me tight without saying a word. It was cold, and we were both shaking as we got back into the car.

Then it was my turn. I took Dad to my Grandma's grave. She had died almost four years earlier, and we buried her on Christmas Eve, her favorite day of the year. I still missed my Grandma very much, and began crying at the grave as I always did. I walked quickly back to the car, and my father followed behind me. He turned on the car heater because I was shivering. He handed me some napkins to dry my face and drove slowly through the cemetery. Dad was quiet for a few moments and then said, "Kelly, you carry around so much pain." Through the sobs, I agreed with him. There were a few more moments of silence as he made a turn, and then he stopped the car. He looked at me with a father's tenderness that was still new to me and said, "You need to let go of the pain from the past."

I started sobbing harder. That was why I wanted to find my father. Finding answers to the past was going to heal the pain—at least, that's what I had expected. Through my sobs I replied, "I don't know how."

He reached for my hand and looked me in the eye and said, "I do, and I'll show you how."

His eyes never left mine, and I could see something in his eyes that I had never seen before—hope.

Before taking him to the airport, we went to a restaurant where we discussed the need for me to start a recovery program. He gave me some ideas on how to find the phone numbers I needed and told me that he'd support me in any way he could. Neither of us ate much that morning. The clock was ticking, and our time was coming to an end.

Unconditional Love

Before we left the restaurant, my father said these profound words to me: "I want you to know that I'm so sorry for the pain that I've caused in your life, and I hope that some day you'll find it in your heart to forgive me." Not only was my father taking responsibility for his mistake, but he asked me for forgiveness! No one who had ever caused me pain had asked to be forgiven. It was at this moment that I felt the unconditional love of a father!

When it was time to say goodbye, we held each other very tight. Through the tears I said the words I have always said in my dreams, "Please, Daddy,

please don't go." But this wasn't a dream, this was reality. We both had lives we needed to get back to.
Even though I *felt* five years old, I was 26 with three
children of my own who needed me to be Mommy.
After my father left, I spent the rest of the day in
tears. I cried because I wanted to go with him. I
wanted him to help me get better. I wanted him to
comfort me when I was scared, dust me off when I
fell, and encourage me when I wanted to quit. But I
had to stay. My life today was with my husband and
children, and it was up to me to make it work. God
had begun to answer my childhood prayers, but I
still had to do my part.

As an abused child years ago, I sat on a bathroom
floor begging God to send my real daddy home to
save me. I thought He wasn't listening. Now I believe
God couldn't allow my father into my life until he
was healthy enough to rescue me.

The next day I started down the road of recovery,
thanks to the intervention of my earthly father and
answered prayer by my heavenly One.

Chapter Five

The Process of Recovery

The day after my father left, I spent the morning on the phone, calling some of the place he had suggested in order to get help. Therapy is expensive, and at that point in my life, I didn't have extra money to spend on a therapist. So, I called the 800 number listed in the phone book for Alcoholics Anonymous and explained I was a sexual abuse survivor and had no idea where to look for help. Soon I was connected with someone who was a survivor herself. She told me that sexual abuse survivor meetings were hard to find in our area. Many had disbanded because a large number of survivors also use drugs and alcohol to numb the pain. And since there were numerous 12-step programs for these problems, people learned to deal with their past abuse through them. I was given number after number until I finally reached Julie who worked for the Porter County Prosecutor's Office in Valparaiso, Indiana. Through the prosecutor's office, she facilitated a group for survivors free of charge. I talked with her for a short time and met with her that afternoon. Julie gave me materials to read, explained the group guidelines, safety issues, etc. I gave her a hug and left both hopeful and fearful at the same time.

The next week I anxiously attended my first meeting. At that point, I had no idea that I would spend the next three years of my life dedicated to recovery from sexual abuse. I thought I'd finish in a few months. I was far too optimistic. One of the important lessons I learned was that recovery is a *process*. My father entering my life was just a part of the process. He had to be healthy to help me and guide me. In recovery, I call this God's timing. It's His way of taking an ugly situation and, in time, turning it into good.

Learning Patience

A process also takes patience. This is something that doesn't come natural to me—I wanted to be better *right now*. I had been in pain long enough.

Yesterday was not soon enough for me to be healed. So, I tried to fix myself in a day. I read the first chapter of *The Courage to Heal* by Laura Davis and Ellen Bass and finished the first 50 pages in the workbook in an hour. I was going to whiz right through recovery, or so I thought.

The result of this "microwave recovery" was that I immediately fell to pieces. I had ripped scabs off scars that were so deep and so old that my "lifeblood" gushed out when they were opened up. I had no idea how to stem the tide of despair. I sat at my table unable to move, overcome with sadness and pain. I felt more hopeless than ever before. If this was recovery, I wanted out. I called my dad, the only person I really trusted who could understand where I was coming from, and begged him to come back and save me. I reminded him that he started me on this road, and I needed him to hold my hand the whole way. "Help me fix this. Take the pain away."

Dad, in the wisdom he learned from his own experience, told me he couldn't fix it for me even though he would like to be able to, but he pointed me toward God. It didn't sound like the best advice at the time, but it would prove to be the golden key for me later. My dad told me to put the book down and not read another page because I was bleeding to death emotionally. We talked until I felt better. He suggested I get busy with something to take my mind off the abuse until I could get to a meeting and share my feelings with people qualified to help. I reluctantly hung up the phone and decided to take a bath...a very long bath. I put on my warm pajamas and snuggle socks even though it was early evening. I made a cup of warm cocoa, curled up under a blanket, and watched *Willy Wonka and The Chocolate Factory* with my kids.

Recovery Takes Time

The first lesson I needed to learn was that healing is a process. I realized that recovery takes time, and I needed to be patient with myself. I learned that the only person who could walk with me on my path toward healing was God. Others can give support, but God is the only one who can carry me when I need it. It was my first experience with this lesson, but not one I would easily accept. It would take me some time to thoroughly understand it.

I also learned that warmth meant comfort to me. I would spend much of my time in pajamas during the next year or so. Is this good or bad? I'm not sure. It was just what I did. Chocolate also became my very best friend. You have to be sober to work a recovery program; that was one of our group guidelines. However, there was nothing in the guidelines about chocolate. Is this good or bad? Again, I'm not sure. At the time it was what I felt I needed.

I began to *walk,* not *run,* down the path of recovery—sometimes very slowly. At times I even
stopped and sat emersed in the pain for awhile.
Familiar pain can be more comfortable because it is
familiar. Sometimes I wondered: *without this pain,
who am I?*

I attended weekly meetings where I shared, listened, and learned. My path to recovery could be
viewed as occurring in three phases—each took me
about a year to complete. For others, it may happen
differently. The three sections in my recovery were:
SORTING, FEELING, and RESOLVING. After I had
worked through them, I would be well on my way to
a healthy life.

*How did I discover the individual
pieces of my pain and then actually sort
them? Through journaling.
Writing down all the details of my
pain on paper saved my life.*

CHAPTER SIX

Sorting the Problems

I love closets. I can take anything I don't want to see, throw it into the deep darkness that holds all my unwanted "stuff," and close the door tight. Visitors to our home are never aware of the mess in my closet. It's a safe place to hide the things I don't want to deal with yet.

I did the same thing with the pain from my childhood sexual abuse. I threw it deep within the closet of my soul and bolted the door so that no one, not even myself, could see it. I had locked in the memory, the anger, and the rage, and had never allowed it to be opened until now. When I began my recovery, I opened the door, set aside the rage and anger, and turned on the light. With fear in my heart, I sat down and began the task of *sorting*.

Sorting

It was a time to be honest with myself. It was a time to label abuse as abuse and not give my abuser an excuse or alibi. I would spend many nights going through the pain. Sorting was hard. I began to find things that I had forgotten were there—other abusers who hurt me, the date rape I experienced, and other secrets I had told no one. They were all buried in this closet of memories. I took them out one by one. Then I put each piece into a particular pile until I was surrounded by many different piles of past pain.

How did I discover the individual pieces of my pain and then actually sort them? Through journaling. Writing down all the details of my pain on paper saved my life. I literally sorted my pain into piles of paper and then put each pile into a different folder. What were the results? When I saw all the details of each particular pain gathered together in one place, I finally recognized it for what it was.

My soul ached from being abused by my stepfather and abandoned by my father. My self-esteem was destroyed when my mother treated my pain as nothing. I felt as though I was to blame for it all.

During the sorting process, I learned to put the blame where it belonged—on the abusers—and that I was not responsible for my abuse.

During the sorting process, I also realized that I was not crazy. I finally understood the ways in which I coped with all my pain through the years; and, even though some of it wasn't pretty, it kept me alive. I learned that the times in high school when I had no idea what day it was, or what class I was going to, or how I got where I was, has a name—it's called dissociation. I learned that spacing out, overeating, drinking alcohol, rationalizing, denying, forgetting, having sex, lying, and even suicide attempts were just a few of the ways I learned to cope with the deep blackness inside.

I was not a bad person; I was just trying to survive—nothing more and nothing less. After a year of sorting my pain—now appropriately labeled—it was time to move on. Where to go from here? The process of my recovery took me to the next stage where I dealt with my feelings.

CHAPTER SEVEN

Uncovering the Feelings

Have you ever been in pain for so long, that after awhile, you don't even really feel it anymore? That's what sexual abuse is like. It's a constant feeling of pain deep within; and, after awhile, the pain becomes familiar, almost normal.

I once described recovery to someone like this: Imagine you have a cut—not a tiny cut but a deep gash in your leg that hurts very badly. Instead of going to the doctor for aid, you hide it under your clothes and ignore its presence. In a short time, you feel the pain of that wound in everything that you do. As you walk, sit, and bend, the pain is with you from morning till night. The pain sometimes awakens you from a deep sleep in the middle of the night. After a period of neglect, the wound becomes an infection that is carried by your bloodstream throughout your entire body. The large gash in your leg became life-threatening because it was ignored in the beginning and never healed properly.

It's the same with sexual abuse. It produces a large wound, not only to the body, but also to the very soul of the victim. The pain was hidden and accepted as a part of life. The wound was present in every thought and decision and choice you made. The pain from the wound is the reason you walk with your head hanging down. You don't want to make eye contact with anyone for fear someone may see the pain. The pain is the reason you sit at the back of the classroom or sleep half the day away. The pain wakes you from deep sleep in the middle of the night over and over again, and you hear the voice of your abuser calling your name in your dreams.

Even in adulthood, the pain infects every part of your life. It lies behind your reason to get married, have children, need alcohol to deaden your feelings, use food to fill the deep void inside, and create a large body to protect you from further abuse. When the pain becomes so deep and so overwhelming that it threatens your very life, the idea of committing suicide becomes almost acceptable.

Where does recovery come into the story? Well, let's now say that you decide not to ignore the pain of the wound anymore. After many weeks of neglect, you take this wound to a doctor. The doctor sees the wound and cleans it with antiseptic—the antiseptic in recovery is the *sorting*. To kill the infection, the doctor will also prescribe some very strong antibiotics. The antibiotics are the *feelings* in recovery. You have to *feel* the pain in order to kill the infection of sexual abuse in your life. You might think that pain is all that you felt from the sexual abuse. I thought the same thing until I started working on some exercises to deal with my feelings.

In the *Courage to Heal* book mentioned earlier, there is a chapter on feelings. It was very strong and difficult to get through. After the first few pages, none of the people in our recovery group wanted to finish the chapter. Our facilitator suggested that we write about why we were afraid of the chapter. This is what I wrote about my feelings:

- I do not believe I deserve to be loved by anyone, not even myself.
- I'm overweight. I'm nothing. I'm ugly, and I'm worthless.
- I feel ashamed of myself.
- I hate the way I look outside, so I hate the way I am on the inside.
- I still feel dirty and ashamed.

I was afraid of this chapter because it forced me to face all of my feelings. I was afraid that my feelings might be wrong; and, therefore, the debasing things my abusers said about me were wrong, too. It was possible that I was not the ugly, worthless child they had said I was. If so, it meant that an innocent child was abused and beaten, and my entire idea of who I am would have to change. I will have to change years of self-hate and self-abuse, which brings up a lot of fear. Who am I? How do I find out? What if I don't like the person I find? *I'm afraid of the person I have buried under all this pain.*

This writing exercise helped me see that I was still blaming myself. Did you notice the part where I wrote about the "ugly, worthless child"? I was still giving the abuser an excuse. But no child deserves to be molested—not even me. My feelings of self-blame gave way to an enormous amount of anger. Now, instead of blaming myself, I blamed everyone. I blamed my stepfather for starting the abuse; I blamed my mother for ignoring it. I blamed my father for deserting me and leaving me in hell. I blamed my family for never seeing it. I even blamed God for not stopping it.

Anger toward others became a new and somewhat "freeing" feeling for me. I was no longer angry at myself for letting it happen. I was angry at everyone else. I knew my anger was getting out of control when I started becoming angry with men in general (men, specifically, because I only knew abuse from them).

After a few mean letters to my dad and some hideous fights with my husband, I decided that I needed more help and began to look for individual assistance. My group meetings were great, but I needed help with the really deep issues on a one-to-one basis. I found a therapist, named Lynne, at Lutheran Social Services. (See the appendix for the helpful information she shares.) Lynne gave me the tools I needed to help me feel what I needed to feel without becoming angry at the entire world.

Distorted Thinking

Lynne taught me about "Cognitive Distortions" listed below. They are the most empowering and healing tools I was given in recovery.

1) ALL OR NOTHING THINKING: You see things in black or white. If your performance is less than perfect, you see yourself as a failure.

2) OVERGENERALIZATION: You see a single negative event as a never-ending pattern of defeat.

3) MENTAL FILTER: You pick out a single negative detail and dwell on it exclusively so that your vision of all reality becomes darkened.

4) DISQUALIFYING THE POSITIVE: You reject positive experiences by insisting they do not count for some reason or other. In this way, you can maintain a negative belief.

5) JUMPING TO CONCLUSIONS: You make a negative interpretation even though there are no definite facts that convincingly support your conclusion.

6) MAGNIFICATION OR MINIMIZATION: You exaggerate the importance of things (e.g., a mistake you made) or you inappropriately shrink things until they appear tiny (i.e., your own good qualities).

7) EMOTIONAL REASONING: You assume that your negative emotions are the way things are. "I feel it, therefore, it must be this way."

8) SHOULD STATEMENTS: You try to motivate yourself with *shoulds* and *shouldn'ts*: should have, could have, would have, have to, ought to, must, can't and won't.

9) LABELING AND MISLABELING; This is an extreme form of overgeneralization. Instead of describing your error, you attach a negative label to yourself. "I am nothing. I am ugly."

10) PERSONALIZATION: You see yourself as the cause of some negative external event which, in fact, you were not primarily responsible for.

A New Program

What I learned from Lynne was that the sexual abuse not only affected my body and my soul, it also affected my thought processes. The mind is amazing. It can only do what it is programmed to do with the information it has been given.

I needed a new program, and Lynne was determined to make sure I had a healthy one. She suggested that I keep a journal of my thoughts and label the cognitive distortions in order to redirect my thought process. I learned from my journal that I started most of my sentences with the words *always, never, everyone,* and *no one.* In other words, I used "all or nothing" thinking. Does anyone *always* or *never* do anything? Of course not.

I also came to realize that I overlooked many of my positive characteristics because I was overweight. I often wrote "I hate myself" (labeling and overgeneralization). The two big ones I learned were Should Statements and Emotional Reasoning. I learned that *shoulda, coulda,* and *woulda* doesn't work. I can't change the past. No one can. I also learned the difference between feelings and facts. Just because you *feel* one way *does not* always mean it's true. I didn't feel my dad loved me when, in reality, he did. I didn't feel special, but I was. I began to understand that feelings were not always an accurate gauge of reality.

Earlier I said that I became angry with my stepfather for starting the abuse. Those feelings were accurate. However, I blamed my mom for ignoring it. Did she ignore it, or did she just not know how to help me? In her generation, the answer was not to talk about it, and it would go away. She just followed conventional wisdom in dealing with me. I blamed my dad for leaving me. He did leave. However, he thought he was doing the best thing for me. He was a drug addict and thought I would be better off without him. At the time, he was probably right. I even blamed God for the abuse. How could that be true? I found it easy to get angry with God because I knew in my heart that when I was done being angry, He would be right there for me. He never left me, not once. It's easier to blame God for the abuse than to put the blame where it belongs—on the abuser.

My pain had lessened after this year, but it was still very present. So I began to ask questions. Where do you put this pain? How do you rid yourself of it forever? How can you make it lose all its power? How do you find the resolve to keep going? I felt that I needed more tools to resolve these issues.

I tried forgetting the pain of abuse. Trust me: if it

worked, I would have stuck with it. The reality is that forgetting doesn't work. I tried so hard to bottle up my feelings, and the result was I became numb to them. I didn't feel anything; I didn't *want* to feel anything; I was *afraid* to feel anything. However, all of the resulting numbness kept me from experiencing joy. If I couldn't feel the bad, I just as surely couldn't feel the good, so I chose to feel nothing. My way of coping was draining the life from me. It was as if I were standing on the outside looking in. I had become a spectator of my own life. Not only had I lost yesterday, I was going to lose today as well.

I have always cried easily. Tears were my body's way of letting out some of the pain. I cried just enough so that I wouldn't explode. I had always thought it was a sign of weakness when I dissolved into a puddle of tears. I would get so angry with myself. As a young child, I was given the impression that tears didn't matter. When I cried for mercy from my stepfather, he never heard a word or acknowledged one tear. The tears meant nothing to him. The only way I could cope as a child was to stuff the feelings of fear, anger, rage, sadness, and despair deep down inside myself.

I may not have been able to control the tears, but I could control what I allowed myself to feel. I determined as a young child to remain in control no matter what the cost. For many years, I *did not* and *would not* feel. After a lifetime of not feeling, the question was: How do I begin to feel in a healthy way once again? I was familiar with depression and hopelessness, but how does feeling make it any better? I thought that recovery meant making the pain go away, not bringing it back. What was the purpose of going back and feeling all the pain? How could that help?

My father had said to me, "Through struggle comes growth." At the time, I had no idea what he meant by that. I would soon learn. *Getting in touch with your feelings means paying attention to what is going on inside you and acknowledging it, instead of pretending it doesn't exist.*

*I'm lucky to have a father who is
familiar with recovery. Of course, he
couldn't fulfill all of my inner child's
wishes. However, he did do things to help
my inner child grow. He said, "I love you"
at the end of every phone call.*

CHAPTER EIGHT

Going Through the Piles

I took my sorted piles and began to go through each and every one. I wrote about each issue, not only *telling* the story but *feeling* the story. I began to feel yesterday's pain. I would no longer tell my story as an outsider looking in. I shared the pain, sadness, fear, anger, hopelessness, and the worthlessness along with the words that described the scenes of my abuse.

I wrote letters to my abusers that were filled with anger and rage. I described their hideous behavior in detail. I called them names just as they had done to me. I put the blame on them and told them that *they* were responsible for the abuse, not me. I read these letters aloud to God and then destroyed them all. I screamed words full of hatred and felt the anger slowly ease with each rip of the page. Sometimes, I went outside and scattered the torn bits of paper to the wind and said, "This is what is left between you and me. You have no more power in my life. Your fate now lies with God." More often than not, it took several episodes like this before the issue was resolved. First, I went through it and felt the anger. The next time, I felt the sadness and grieved for the child who endured all the pain. Next, I felt the physical symptoms that accompanied it: headache, nausea, pelvic pain, sore arms, and gagging. There were many different feelings attached to each issue, and each needed to be exposed in order to finally deal with it and remove it from my life.

My Inner Child

Our group therapy took us through many writing exercises including some "child within" work. This was creative as well as helpful. It helped me see that small child who was abused as myself, not as a picture or an anonymous face. She was me. The child within work is difficult, but it's well worth the effort.

We once did a project for the child within that had two parts. The first part was to write a letter to yourself as a little girl. My inner child was screaming for her daddy. She wanted him to hold her and make all the pain go away. She wanted him to be near her and help her feel safe. She wanted to spend time with him every day. This inner child began to get on my nerves; some of the things she wanted were impossible. I had found my Dad, but he lives in Florida and I live in Indiana, which poses a bit of a problem. Daily lunches and Sunday afternoons at Daddy's were just not going to happen. The child within wanted to hear his voice every day. She wanted him because he made her feel safe. In her eyes, *I* had even betrayed *her*. *I* had blamed *her* for letting the abuse happen. She didn't even really trust me. She only wanted Daddy. So, I wrote her this letter.

I'm sorry you endured so much pain for so long. I want you to know that I do not blame you anymore. It wasn't your fault. I know that you still don't completely trust me. However, I think we are building a good foundation. I know that you still want Daddy to make it all better, and believe me, I wish he could, but he can't. The best I can do for you is to allow you as much communication with him as you need. I know it's not the same as snuggling into his arms and feeling safe and protected, but it is really the best I can do.

I held up my end of the bargain. I'm lucky to have a father who is familiar with recovery work and who also participated in it. Of course, he couldn't fulfill all of my inner child's wishes. He didn't move to Indiana. He didn't always call when he was supposed to. He didn't write very often, and he was busy living his own life. However, he did do some things to help my inner child grow. He said, "I love you" at the end of every phone call. My inner child wanted him close to her, so I asked him to purchase a stuffed animal that resembled his personality. He found one and put some of his cologne on it so it smelled like him. My inner child held onto this "daddy bear" for quite some time. Dad mailed her an Easter basket filled with candy and a stuffed bunny. When I spent the week with him, he held my hand, took me to the zoo, kissed my cheek, and hugged me good night.

My inner child wanted my Dad to be the Daddy she dreamed about and wished for. However, my therapist warned me about illusions. Illusions have no faults. In her imagination, she could wish him to do anything, and he would. However, in reality, my Dad was a real person made of flesh, bones, and flaws. Just like any child, when her needs weren't met, she threw a fit. However, just like other children, she began to grow up and accept reality at face value—no more magical thinking. She had a choice to accept Daddy for who he was or hold onto an illusion that would never happen. In time, my inner child chose Dad, even with his faults.

Connecting the Inner and Outer Self

The goal of the second part of the project was to connect the outside me with the inside me. Survivors of sexual abuse see themselves cut off from their bodies. Their bodies have very little emotional value—they're just a wall of protection to keep the outside world from harming the fragile soul inside. The "inside me" was vulnerable, small, innocent, gentle, and beautiful—totally different from the "outside me."

In order to accomplish this, we used an empty box and some magazines. With the lid on, the box represented the outside me. However, with the lid off, I could see the inside me. We cut out pictures and words from the magazines and glued them both inside and outside the box. My box had very large eyes on the lid with a tear streaming down, representing all the tears I had unwillingly shed. I found a picture of long, brown, beautiful hair. It was the only thing I like about the outside me. I cut out many words that spelled *fat*. I pasted them all around the sides of the box, depicting my wall against harm. I added a picture of a chocolate doughnut—my drug of choice. I also pasted a large smile on the top of the box with the eyes and hair. The smile represented the mask I wore for so long. No matter what the pain was—I smiled. That was the way I got through it. *Nothing of real value went on the outside of the box.*

The inside me was very different. On the inside, I had a girl about the age of eight swinging on a swing being pushed by her Daddy. She was smiling and you could tell that she was happy and safe. She felt loved and special because her Daddy told her she was. Sunshine and beauty filled the inside of the box except for one small corner that was black. It was empty with only a small angel pasted off to one side. There was still pain here. It would take more time before I would be healed from that pain.

I did a lot of writing, both in and out of group therapy, and I destroyed most of it right after I finished sharing it. Writing my story and my feelings about it became my way of learning how to feel once again. I could write anything because I never kept it. I shredded the pain and threw it away. However, I do have a few pieces of writing that somehow did not get destroyed. One of them is the following exercise on grieving for our losses.

> I have a picture in my mind. It's a small child...a little girl who's small, but her pain is great. Her eyes are wide open watching every move of her abuser, but she can't defend herself, she can only be prepared. Her cries go unheard and her physical symptoms ignored.

The innocence was lost. The belief in family and safety. The beliefs that people were good, children were special, were all taken. Dignity, self-respect, self-worth never existed. I was left with shame, hate, rage, and disgust.

What was lost? I was lost. I never got a chance to exist. At a young age, the person who dwelled inside crawled deep within the body and became a coping identity—an obedient child who tried to please everyone but never could. One who endured hell. She endured the rapes, the physical abuse, the emotional beatings. This false self protected the original child and never let her see or feel the pain of the outside world. It was her job to protect the child inside. That's why she existed. The child that was tucked away died. She died because she never got a chance to play, to love, or to exist. She never got to have a birthday party or a sleep-over. She would look out from time to time and she knew it would never be safe enough to come back. So, she curled up into a ball way back in a small part of my soul where she sits frozen in time. That was my first loss.

The losses go on and on. The body lost form

because it needed to protect itself. The eyes lost their shine from witnessing all the pain. The skin grew numb so as not to feel.

These are some of my losses. What do I grieve? I grieve it all. I grieve for each and every child that endured all of this and more. I grieve for the children who still suffer today. I grieve for that little child buried deep within me. May she someday find safety and peace.

CHAPTER NINE

Resolving Matters

L et's look again at the illustration of the deep wound on the leg. The cut was ignored for a long time so it began to affect every part of life. An infection set in and the person became sicker and sicker. Finally, with no more denial or excuses, it was time for help. The doctor cleaned the wound (sorting—facing the facts). Then he gave antibiotics for the infection (facing the feelings). After much care, medicine, and time, the wound was healed. There's nothing the doctor can do about the large scar that's left. The scar is the memory of the past. The past is always there. Nothing can change it. However, now the scar can be seen and touched and felt without pain. That, my friends, is when you resolve a matter. To resolve is to deal with something successfully. It is looking back at the past for what it was and validating the truth of it, but with the absence of pain.

Let Go and Let God

There *is* life without pain, and I will tell you how I found it. From the beginning of our new relationship, my father told me to go to God with my problems. I have always believed in God and have attended church for years and years. I knew the Bible stories of Noah and how he built the ark, how David killed the giant, and how Daniel was safe in the lions' den. I knew church as a child knows church. However, I was no longer a child, and it was time to become an adult with a deep relationship with God.

During this time of recovery, I attended Sunday School class and learned quite a lot. Don't get the wrong impression; I didn't sit quietly in class. I must have fought every issue we discussed. Why? I didn't really trust God entirely yet. Believing in Him and trusting in Him are two entirely different things.

I still felt abandoned by Him. He had let my stepfather rape me. He watched me get hurt over and over again and did nothing to stop it. What kind of God would allow a child to be hurt like this and do nothing? All those years I felt that my heavenly Father was worse than my earthly father. I thought at least my earthly father had no idea what was going on so he couldn't do anything to stop the abuse. God, however, was there the entire time. Why didn't He do something? How could I trust God? I believed that He had helped the people in the Bible stories because He loved them. For a long time, I believed in my heart that God didn't love me. I felt that God had known all my secrets and despised me for them.

Remember, there is a difference between feelings and facts. God didn't choose for my abuse to happen; my stepfather did. It was my stepfather's choice to hurt me. That's a fact. If anything, it was the absence of God in my stepfather's heart that contributed to my abuse. Putting the blame on God is taking the easy way out. I had to place the blame where it belonged. The people who hurt me deserve the blame—not God.

In recovery, I was struggling with giving my pain over to God. Let go and let God? How do I do that? I was the one who did all the work so far. I was the one who did all the sorting, wrote all the letters, did all the journaling, and read all the books. I have been in control of fixing myself for so long. How do I turn the control over to God? The answer? One day at a time. For me it was even a little smaller than that...one moment at a time...one issue at a time. I started small and after God "earned" some of my trust, I allowed Him a little more of my life.

Knowledge is power. If I didn't know how to do something, I found the information that I needed. I began my search by reading the Bible outside the walls of the church building. I began praying—and not just before meals and bedtime. I kept praying and asking God to show me He was there with me. "Help me trust you. I still feel so abandoned by You. Help me feel safe within Your arms," I prayed. I soon found out that God *does* answer prayer. My husband bought me a wonderful book entitled *Daddy Loves His Girls* by Bishop T.D Jakes. It was written by a man in honor of his daughters. I cried through every chapter. My heart was so touched by his poignant writing that I just could not put it down.

One night, I was trying to finish a chapter in bed when my husband came in. He asked me if he could turn off the light. I said yes, but I really didn't mean yes. After about ten minutes of laying there quietly, I took my book, crept into our bathroom, and shut the door. I sat on the side of the tub in the dim light and read about fatherless daughters. In this chapter, Bishop Jakes describes fathers as a necessity. When an earthly father is not present, there's pain in the daughter's life. He explains that God's plan is for both parents to be there to assist in the nurturing of the girl. He describes how girls search for answers about men from their fathers. He also talks about the tragedy of the molested girl and how she needs to understand that sex is different than love. His love for his daughters spills over the pages of the book. I was touched in a way I had never been by anything I had ever read.

Love Conquers Pain

Was there really supposed to be such love between fathers and daughters? More importantly, was there such love between the brokenhearted and abandoned little girl and her heavenly Father? My eyes were so full of tears the words on the pages began to blur. I read aloud to God: "What can she do? She has cried; she has prayed. She lies on the floor like a bird whose broken wing has stopped the flight that should have been. She sings her song from the ground. Her helpless flapping comes out as temper tantrums, mood swings, addictive behavior, or compulsive affairs. She is miserable. She is trapped. She ages, grays, and becomes weaker without becoming wiser. Trapped in a time warp, she relives little girl issues in a woman's body. She is trapped between ages and stages of life—too much of a woman to be a little girl, but too much of a little girl to be a woman."

I fell to my knees sobbing. Tears ran down my face and my nose was wet with sadness from the past. I said aloud to God: "Do you hear this? Do you hear the pain?" I continued reading, and as I read, I trembled with sadness and sorrow. I tried to read to myself, but I couldn't. It was a story that God and I had to read together. I wanted Him to hear the words from a mouth filled with pain.

The book continued, "What can she do? How can she break free? She needs to understand that all men are not the same. Isolating the problem brings healing. Like a cancer, it must be isolated and removed. Second, she must allow God's love to pierce through the pain. It must be God's love first. God's love is the only love that is perfect enough to pass her stringent test. His love will restore to her the opportunity for the little girl in her to have a loving relationship with a Father who will not fail. Love is God's gift given against pain. She can come right now and lay her head upon His strong breast and be healed. There is no molestation in God; He will not abuse her. She can trust Him."

I dropped the book to the floor. I was crying and shaking, and I felt so cold and alone. It was in that moment that I felt a warmth come over me once again. My eyes closed; I was so overwhelmed. Here I was reading out loud so that God would hear my pain, and somehow God turned it around and began talking to me so I could hear His love for me. I was His child and He loved me. The warmth continued to fill my body and the coldness left. Through the sobs I heard the words, "I never left you!" My heavenly Father loved me, and I could trust Him. He will never abandon me. My inner child was right—it would take a Daddy to make all the pain go away.

Chapter Ten

Practicing Recovery

During the next two years, I started to become very active in practicing my recovery. Group therapy is great—going to all the meetings, sitting with one another, and sharing your thoughts and feelings. However, the real change begins to happen when you actually take an active role in your own recovery. It's not real until you begin to get off your backside, so to speak, work the exercises, and use the new tools in your everyday life.

I began journaling every day. In the evenings, I wrote down what happened each day, whether it was

good, whether it was bad, or whether it wasn't anything special at all. I wrote so that I could see what I
was doing and if I had made any progress that day. In
that way, I acknowledged my feelings and didn't ignore them. I worked at putting my feelings and my
body together to make them one instead of separate,
as I had always done before recovery.

I learned to enjoy the little things in life. When I
took the children to the park, instead of staying in
the car, I'd sit on the swings and talk with them.
Sometimes I closed my eyes and let my inner child
play a little bit as I pumped the swing higher and
higher. We packed picnic lunches and had great fun
eating them there. On the outside, I might have
looked like the mom, but my little inner child was
having a great day with my family.

It was important to me that I labeled and validated my feelings. If I felt angry or discouraged about
not quickly healing from the past, if I felt frustrated
with still having to deal with some of the issues of
sexual abuse, I wrote them down. I made sure that I
actively paid attention to my life and my feelings so
that the healing could continue. I began to meditate
and pray. I took time to get in touch with who I am
on the inside. I allowed God into my heart, soul, and
spirit so He could continue to heal me. Then I began
to keep a prayer journal and write down what I med-
itated on. I found that certain music helped my mind

focus on soothing thoughts and the wonderful warmth of God's healing power that worked within me.

I exercised the new, healthy coping skills that I learned in recovery. Now when I became agitated and began to feel some of the body memories of the abuse, I could do something about them. If I began to gag, I marched into the bathroom and brushed my teeth. If I began to feel pain in my pelvic area, I lit a candle and took a bubblebath. And, yes, I told the inner child, "I know you hurt today. Since we've learned how to soothe some of this pain, let's soothe it." Instead of pushing it away, I brought it to the surface and acknowledged it, and it would leave. If the same issue came up a couple of days later, I dealt with it all over again. The more often I practiced these steps, the less often the pain would come back.

I also wrote positive affirmations every day. I had believed lies for so long that I didn't really *feel* anything good about myself. I began to *speak* positive words about myself even if I didn't feel them. I wrote, "I am a valuable person, I am a valuable person" over and over and over again. "I deserve to enjoy a happy and healthy life. I am not responsible in any way for being abused." I wrote these words in my journal many times. The more that I wrote them, the more I began to believe them. I was becoming convinced about them in my mind. Everything I had been convinced of in the past was a lie. "I *am* a valuable person. I *am* a valuable person." I said it over and over again. And the lies began to melt away.

Participating in Life

At first, I didn't know how to participate in my life—I didn't know what it meant to be a mother or a wife. I didn't know who I was. If I'm not a survivor, if I'm not choking on the pain of yesterday, then who am I? Who am I today? I began to participate in my life and enjoy each day. The first step was *staying in the moment*. From the time I woke up in the morning, I tried to focus on staying in the moment. Today is all I have, so I began to stay in today and live for today and not tomorrow. So many times I used to think, "You know, if I could just make it till tomorrow, I would be okay." Now I began *living for today* instead of *hoping for tomorrow*. I began taking action *today* so that *today* would be beautiful. And slowly, as I learned to put all this into practice, I began to smile—not just the smile that you put on when you're in pain and say, "Oh, everything's fine." No, not that kind of smile. I began to smile from the inside out. I was feeling that smile inside, and I was beginning to feel what I had never felt before—a wonderful feeling called joy.

To my inner child who was so used to pain, joy was such an unfamiliar feeling. It may sound funny, but how do you enjoy joy? How do you feel joy when you've never felt it before? It was very strange at first. I sat back and said, "What I'm feeling is not pain—it's happiness!" It felt like there was a warmth inside, and it was that warmth that I had been trying to create with alcohol and food and all my addictions and dissociation. I had tried to stuff all of this into my emptiness to create a feeling of warmth inside me. I finally realized the feeling was happening on its own.

Children

Joy in the moment is what I began to participate in and acknowledge and feel. I saw the value of my life. A funny thing happens when you change the glasses that you're looking through. I took off the glasses of pain, and I put on the glasses of joy. Instead of seeing my children as an overwhelming sense of responsibility that I didn't know how to cope with, I began to see them as the enormous blessings they are and appreciate the sense of joy they could bring into my life.

Another funny thing happened. Earlier when I was stuck in all that pain, I used to say that the only reason I got out of bed was for my kids. The only reason that I stayed alive in this world was for my kids. Now instead of living *for* my children, I began to live *with* my children. I began to participate and enjoy life with them instead of just saying, "It's all I can do just to be here." Just being here is not enough. Children need you to participate in their lives and to be active with them. And that's what I was now doing. Before, I was only there *physically;* I wasn't there *emotionally.* I'd go to their soccer games and sit in the chair on the sidelines. The game went on right in front of me, but instead of cheering for my kids, my mind would take me to a different place. The pain of yesterday would creep in and steal my today. I vowed that I would no longer let the pain of childhood steal any more todays with my family.

I began to be active with them. I began to participate physically *and* emotionally in their lives. I took an interest in their school—not just checking their homework when they were done, but I became a "room mom." And even though it's a lot of work to make cupcakes and treats every few weeks, and plan all the holiday parties, it was well worth it for me and for them.

I went on school field trips; I visited the apple orchard with my son's class. We picked apples and came home and peeled them to make pie together. It created a warmth inside me. Joy was healing my spirit. We did a lot of other things together. I discovered a wonderful new world, not only for my children but also for myself. Even though I read storybooks to them in the past, before I just read the words; I never felt the joy of the story. Now I read these wonderful stories to my kids and participated with them both physically and emotionally.

The healing joy continued to spread through me. We played games, and I did it because I *wanted to* participate with them. When you play a game with the children, and you're there both physically and emotionally, you're given this wonderful opportunity to communicate with them that you can't get any other way. They're so willing to let you into their lives.

Now they were excited to come home and tell me all about their day. All three of them would bubble over with their day all at once, and I had to make them take turns. They were so excited because I think, even though they probably didn't realize it, there was a difference in me and they responded to it. They could see in my eyes that I had an interest in them and was concerned about every little thing in their lives. I wanted to be there for them. And they were so willing to let me in.

When my daughter came home from school, she told me who said what to whom, and what boy likes what girl, and what girl likes what boy, and what boy she liked. And then we went to get my son who was into games that were "cool." And that's what we'd talk about with him. I learned to enter this wonderful realm of their lives, and I knew it was a blessing, opportunity, and privilege to be a part of it.

I watched my youngest daughter, who is naturally so full of joy, bounce around with a smile that's always on her face because of the security she has in who she is and the safety that surrounds her. I saw that her innocent joy and happiness was what I wanted all along. I watched how she willingly allowed me to hold her and comfort her and how she took such happiness from those hugs and kisses. I could sense the safety that she felt in her relationship with us as parents. I began to watch her, and I learned from my children how to feel joy in life.

Marriage

I also learned to be an active participant in my marriage. I got married to jump out of a very bad situation. (I've met many survivors who have done the same thing—it tends to be a common denominator.) My thinking through the "happily ever after" and "Prince Charming" thing was that I had endured hell, surrounded by emotional, physical, and sexual abuse for so long, that I believed nothing could be worse. And no matter what happened, no matter what the arguments were, no matter what the difficulties were, nothing could be worse than where I was. So getting married would be easy. How wrong I was! I was totally unprepared to become a wife and mother. I did so to fill up the empty gap inside of me, but it didn't work. You can't absorb the joy from someone else. You have to heal so that joy can fill you up, too. I needed to become emotionally, as well as physically, involved with my husband.

I used to think that Joe was just like all other men, that he was dangerous, that he only wanted one thing—sex. I figured he would leave eventually just like all the other men in my life had done. I believed that I couldn't let him get close to me because if I allowed my heart to be vulnerable to him, he could hurt me. That's all I've ever known. I tried to crucify my husband for all the pain that other men caused me. I considered the male species as the "enemy" because of my abusers. But I was wrong. I was so wrong. I held Joe responsible for the actions of the people who hurt me when, in reality, he had nothing to do with it. If anything, he wanted to help me. He tried so often to help me, but he couldn't because no one could heal me but God. The pain of sexual abuse could only be healed through my cooperation with God's grace.

I was great at fighting. I knew exactly what to say to hit him right where it hurt the most. I knew where his weak spots were because he had made himself vulnerable to me. I knew what words would cause him—a gentle, kind man—to get so furious that he had to leave the house. I knew what to say, and I chose to say it because I felt that was what fighting was all about—hurting the other person as much as you could. And I was good at it.

Joe and I had been married ten years, and I was still throwing his ex-girlfriend in his face. Ten years of marriage, and I still felt jealous of a young girl he dated when he was 16 years old. I threw this phrase at him, "Well, you should have married the blonde." But, you know, that wasn't fair. That wasn't fair to Joe at all.

I kept Joe at arm's length from me. I kept him there because I believed he would eventually leave me. My family doesn't have a very good batting average when it comes to marriage. And, to be honest with you, I haven't had the opportunity to get to know many happily married couples. My mom was divorced twice. My father was in his third marriage, having been divorced twice. Even my grandmother was divorced. So my perception of marriage was that it eventually ended—only a lucky few could make it last. I kept Joe at a distance so that when he did leave, it wouldn't hurt so much.

I was jealous of Joe, too. I watched the way that he held our children. I saw the way he naturally had fun and enjoyed these little people we have in our lives. The sparkle in his eyes and the smile on his face was amazing to me, and I was jealous of it. He came by it so naturally. I had no clue how to get it.

What I didn't see was that he also looked at me with that same love and tenderness, but I wouldn't accept it. He told me I was beautiful, and he loved me. I rolled my eyes and my response to him was, "Yeah, right." I didn't believe him.

I used to complain, saying that if Joe changed this or that about himself, our marriage would be better. Now, it was time for *me* to change. Now, it was time for me to take all the new relational skills that I had learned, step up to the plate, and take my "turn at bat." I needed to put all of me into this marriage. I needed to not just be in this marriage physically, but to be involved in this marriage emotionally as well. Making the decision to do this was much easier than actually doing it. How do you become a wife? I was never taught how to love a husband. For example, we had a saying in my house when I was growing up that 99.9 percent of all men are jerks. My childhood never prepared me for marriage.

My old way of thinking was that if I kept the house clean, cooked the meals, and was a good mother to the children—juggling all the soccer matches, baseball practices, and Sunday School classes for the kids—and did the laundry and ironing, I was *showing* Joe that I loved him. I was physically involved and I was participating, and I thought that was enough. But it's *not* enough. I needed to become an active participant in my marriage, both physically *and* emotionally.

Now, knowledge is power. If you don't know how to be a good wife, how do you learn to be one? That's the question I began to ask myself.

*Joe and I made a conscious decision
to put our individual walk with God first,
our marriage second, and our kids third.
What is amazing is that the closer
Joe and I drew to God, the closer
we drew to each other.*

CHAPTER ELEVEN

What Is Love?

At this stage in my recovery, when I was searching for how to become the wife I needed to be, our Sunday school class began discussing the word *love* as it is described in 1 Corinthians 13 in which the apostle Paul gives the classic definition of love.

> *Love is patient and love is kind. It does not envy. It is not boastful. It is not proud. It's not rude. It's not self-seeking, not easily angered, keeps no record of wrongs, does not delight in evil but rejoices in the truth, always pro-*

tects, always trusts, always hopes, always perseveres, and love never fails (v. 4-8).

Many of us have heard those words before and thought, "Yeah, okay, that's how it should be in a perfect world." But aren't these attributes of love what we all need to have? I came to the realization that love isn't a noun. Love is a verb. It's action. Love is actively participating with someone else.

To be patient. What does it mean? Waiting without complaining. *To be kind.* Kindness is the act of seeking the best for another with goodness in your heart. *Not easily angered.* One of the first things that Joe and I decided to work hard at in this stage of my recovery was knowing how to fight. Now, that may sound strange to some people. When you get married, it's not *if* you're going to argue; it's *when* you're going to argue. When you put two people together, whether they're husband and wife, brother and sister or friends, there's eventually going to be conflict. The important thing is to know how to have conflict in a healthy way.

One of the healthiest decisions Joe and I made at this time was making it an ironclad rule that *the divorce word would never be said* in our house during any argument, ever. The first six years of our marriage, we had thrown the "divorce" word around day in and day out. "Well, if you don't like the way things are, then get a divorce." "Go ahead, leave, get a divorce. I don't really care." That word is very damaging and hurtful. In my mind, divorce was an option that was chosen far too easily in my family. So we made the decision that no matter what the argument was about, the divorce word was never to be spoken. No matter what the conflict, we had a commitment to one another that we would work it out. No one was going to quit the relationship.

We also learned *not to go for the jugular*. When we argued about a certain situation, we learned not to throw something that happened ten years ago at each other. We learned to stay in the argument and discuss the real issues. One of the regular arguments we had centered around how much work Joe did outside. When he mowed the yard and did the gardening, I felt he would rather be outside than with me. I wasn't angry because he wanted to go out and mow the yard. That's silly, isn't it? I was hurt because I felt as if I wasn't the number one priority in his life.

As I learned to be a more active participant, both physically and emotionally, in our marriage, I realized that the most important thing I needed to do as a wife was to put Joe before my needs. I'm a "show you" person. I'll show you that I care by doing all the housework, cooking, cleaning, and ironing. *I'm showing that I love you and care about you* through those actions. I needed to learn what Joe needed. I saw that Joe is a "touch me" person. He likes to snuggle on the couch, hold hands, etc. I had to consciously decide to meet his needs instead of worrying so much about how I kept up the house. I also thought that if I was an involved parent and mother to my children that I showed them I loved them. But I learned that the best thing I could do for them was to love their father.

Joe and I had both been guilty of putting our kids first. In Joe's defense, when you have a wife who keeps you at a distance, it's easy to do. He built his relationship with the children and worked hard at it. As I began to use the skills I learned in recovery, I was comfortable being physically and emotionally involved as their mother. But I was also putting them first, and that was wrong. I learned that the best foundation I could build for my children was a healthy, happy marriage.

Joe and I made a conscious decision to put our individual walk with God first, our marriage second, and our kids third. What is amazing is that the closer Joe and I drew to God, the closer we drew to each other.

I had a lot to learn about intimacy. As a survivor of sexual abuse, the first thing that came to my mind when I heard the word "intimacy" was sex. I thought that's all men ever wanted anyway. I learned about the many different types of intimacy. Sexual intimacy should be the end result of the other forms of intimacy. I had to let down my guard and be willing to allow my husband access to my heart. I needed to become vulnerable to him. I worked hard on intimacy. Now I share not only the pain with my husband, but all of my feelings. I let Joe inside to see my vulnerable spots. I rebuilt a commitment to my husband. I finally believed that he was not going to leave me. After all, he had proven for more than 11 years now that he loved me unconditionally.

It took me time to understand all of these principles. Reprogramming my mind with all this new information also took time. Author Gary Smalley has produced an incredible video series recently re-named *Hidden Keys to Loving Relationships*. In these tapes, he talks about the differences between men and women and how we communicate differently.

The tape series exposed to me the lie that all men are cold-hearted, that they are the enemy. It helped me become more emotionally and physically active. After a couple of years of doing this, I began to see exciting results. We attended a convention called Marriage Builders, and it was a very emotional experience for us. It helped build a closer bond between us as we worked really hard on our marriage.

As our marriage improved, other areas of my life

blossomed. I started to enjoy hobbies, and I became involved in various areas of my church and community. I thought *life is good. Life is good. I'm having a great time.* I felt joy deep within my soul for the first time in my life!

One problem remained that needed to be dealt with. It turned out to be the most significant.

CHAPTER TWELVE

The Final Puzzle Piece

Even though I was enjoying life more than I had ever done before, I was still in significant pain. In the darkness of night, I continued to get up and sneak food. I had quit drinking—I had been sober now for years. I had quit smoking—I wanted one almost every day, but I made a deliberate effort for my health's sake to actively nurture myself. So why was I still addicted to overeating? It was the final missing puzzle piece to my total recovery.

Recovery reminded me a little bit of our house. We moved into a beaten up, old house and had to do an enormous amount of work on the exterior. It had rusty white steel siding, and a big, old crumbling cement porch. There was also a side porch that was half falling off. Everything on the house was old. Slowly, we began to remodel it. We started by first installing 25 new windows. We pulled off the old metal siding and replaced it with new vinyl siding. We added new trim painted a beautiful hunter green and built a new wooden deck onto the front of the house. We replaced the old roof with a new deep green one, to match the trim. We tore down the side porch and put a little wooden fence around the back of the yard. When you stand back and look at our house, it looks really good outside, but there were still some things that needed to be done inside before we were finished. But you wouldn't notice them if you just drove past the house.

I had been "driving past" an area of my life for years. One day I took a long look at myself in the mirror. I knew in my head I was not responsible in any way for being abused. I knew without a doubt that I am a valuable person—I was created in the image of God. I worked hard at making all the changes in my life, but I was still abusing myself with food. It dawned on me that day—*there was still an empty spot in my soul.* Joy had filled so much of the hollowness that I didn't think about there being any last empty spot. But there was one place left that needed to be healed. What was it? What was left? I was the only one who could figure out what it was because it was buried deep inside me. In order to discover what it was, I went back to the basics of recovery. While I kept trying to quit using the food to fix the pain, I searched for the answer. After several unsuccessful weeks, I finally realized I was going about it backwards. It wasn't the food that I needed to confront. The food's not my enemy. I had to confront the pain. What was the pain? What was left?

I took my journal out and began to write late one evening. It was just gibberish at first—sadness for this, anger about that, but basically just my everyday dealings with life. My children had fallen asleep hours before, and my husband had also gone to bed. I went to the kitchen and fixed a cup of hot chocolate because chocolate was my "drug" of choice. As I drank it, I hoped its warmth would seep into that deep, dark place inside me. Suddenly, I didn't have to write any more. I knew what it was that was still plaguing me! I took a deep breath and before my eyes flashed a picture of a 16-year-old girl staring at herself in the mirror just after an abortion.

I saw her standing there with her hands clenching the bathroom countertop. I watched her splash water over her face and run her fingers through her long, brown hair. I heard her say these words to the face in the mirror: "I hate you, and I'm

never going to forgive you for what you have done."
All at once, I understood the reason why I still
abused myself with food—I still considered myself
worthless because of the abortion.

CHAPTER THIRTEEN

The Dilemma

The abortion occurred in the middle of my high school years. Bill and I went to the same school. We walked to class, held hands, and ate lunch together everyday. His friends became my friends, and my friends became his friends. We studied together as much as we could. He was really nice to me. He was sweet and gentle and had soft, caring eyes. I really didn't expect to stay with Bill long, but I found myself growing closer and closer to him. He was really a very kind young man.

He was so different from all the other boys I had ever known. He had a lot of respect for his mother.

She worked, and he always cleared the dinner table, rinsed the dishes, and stacked them in the dishwasher for her. He followed their rules carefully and always asked permission before he left the house. He was a good kid, and he was a nice guy. He had a genuine, loving, caring heart. Most importantly, he saw something in me that I certainly didn't see. No one had ever looked at me like he did—his eyes lit up when I walked into the room. He was proud to be my boyfriend. It felt so special; no one had ever made me feel special before.

He was a thin, sandy haired guy who played the guitar. My mother hated that about him because it reminded her of my dad, who played when they first met. During these years, I was active in our church youth group. It was very important to me that Bill and I did the same things together. So he came to youth group with me and played with the Christian band on Thursday nights. We were having a great time.

Bill didn't pressure me into having sex. He had never done it before and wanted to wait until I was ready. I felt very close to him, so we eventually had sex. Not long afterward, the unthinkable happened— I became pregnant. I swear, I was sure it wasn't possible. I'd been sexually abused for so much of my life that I didn't think I could get pregnant. I was surprised, but I knew even before I took the pregnancy test. I confided in Larry, our youth minister, and he took me and my friend, Jennifer, to Planned Parenthood to get the test.

Waiting for the results seemed like an eternity. Finally the woman called me in and told me that the test was positive. Tears started streaming down my cheeks. She asked me what I wanted to do. I said, "I'm going to have this baby, and I'm going to keep it." I didn't think that there was any other option available to me, nor did I want any. She sent me for prenatal counseling, although at the time I didn't understand what that word meant.

I paid the bill, grabbed my coat and purse, and we left. As soon as I got out of the building, I started crying. Deep within my heart, I was afraid. We went to pick up Bill, and I broke the news to him. He started to cry right away. Larry left us alone for a little while, and we just held each other and rocked back and forth. We were so afraid. I think we were more afraid of our parents than anything. Bill's father had a deep, intimidating voice and was very controlling. He used anger to control the people around him, and I know Bill was afraid of him. I was afraid to tell my mother—I thought she might throw me out of the house.

Bill and I were still trying to absorb what was happening to us. We didn't talk about what needed to be done yet. That night we went to a concert at a neighboring church where he played the guitar. My girlfriend and I sat outside in the grass underneath a tree, and we talked and cried about my predicament while the musicians tuned up. Jennifer reached down and found a four-leaf clover for me. I kept it in my wallet for a long time afterward because somehow it gave me a measure of hope. We went into the concert and tried to have a good time.

Afterward, Larry drove the five of us to my house and we sat outside in my front yard. There was Bill and my friend, Jennifer, and Bill's friend, Ralph, Larry and me. All of us were afraid of what was going to happen to Bill and me. I hoped Larry could make the problem go away with some of his infinite wisdom. He always seemed to have the answers to everything. But no one really had an answer for this.

Soon I began to show signs of pregnancy, but I tried to hide it from everyone. I was vomiting every day, and I had cravings. Finally, I mustered the courage to tell my mom. Before she came home from work, I took a small brown paper bag and filled it with some clothes because I was sure she was going to tell me to leave. I eased up behind where she was sitting and blurted out that I had gone to Planned Parenthood with Larry where I had a pregnancy test, and it came out positive. She turned around and looked at me. I think her eyes were full of more fear than mine. She was also very angry.

"So, you're pregnant?"

All I could get out was, "Yes, I am."

She turned her back to me and didn't say anything for a few minutes. Finally she muttered, "I'll call Planned Parenthood tomorrow."

I said, "Mom, I'm not sure what I want to do yet."

She quickly jerked her head back around and shouted, "You're having an abortion!"

I didn't plead or beg with her. I was just grateful that she didn't throw me out of the house. So I went upstairs and fell asleep from total exhaustion.

About a week later, my mom made an appointment at Planned Parenthood. We didn't talk much at all. I could tell she was very angry with me, and she stayed very distant. She was clear that she didn't want to see Bill at our house *ever again.*

Although I didn't want to go to the counselor, we kept the appointment. When my name was called, the lady stopped my mother from coming in and said that she wanted to speak to me alone. So my mother sat down very reluctantly. I was embarrassed being with the counselor because she knew I was pregnant. She had a soft, gentle voice and asked, "What do you want to do about the baby? What are you comfortable with? What do you think is the right thing to do?"

I looked at her and said, "I know I've made a mistake. I know that, but I want to keep the baby. I'll live with my mistake." I was crying softly as I spoke.

She replied, "Okay." She thought that it was that simple. I couldn't believe it! She opened the door and called my mother in.

After my mom had been seated, the counselor began, "Well, Kelly has decided to keep her baby."

My mother exploded, "What do you mean she's decided to keep this baby?" She screamed at the counselor. I was so embarrassed, I began to cry all the more.

The counselor continued, "Kelly realizes she's made a mistake and is responsible enough to say that she wants to deal with that mistake. Maybe we should be really proud of her that she's willing to take responsibility for it."

My mother's rage just intensified. She shouted, "You're supposed to tell her how this is going to mess up her whole life. Tell her how hard it is to raise a child on your own. She's not going to be able to do it. I'm going to have to be the one who will raise this child, and I'm not going to do it!"

She screamed at the counselor to tell me all the facts and change my mind. The counselor just looked at me because I think she was as shocked as I was. My mother grabbed my wrist, pulled me up out of the chair, and we left. She peeled out of the parking lot and drove as fast as I've ever seen her drive. Within minutes we had pulled into the parking lot of the school and she slammed on the brakes.

She yelled at me, "Go ahead, run in and tell him the good news—you're going to keep the baby. Go tell him." I just looked at her with my mouth hanging open. Feeling betrayed by my own mother, I forced the sobs back down my throat. I jerked open the car door and got out as quickly as I could. Slamming the door, I ran into the school brushing hot tears away from my eyes.

The bell was just beginning to ring for lunch so I waited by our locker for Bill because we shared a locker. He put his arm around me and we went out for a walk. We never did go back to class that day. We spent the rest of the afternoon just talking. I poured it all out to him: I didn't want to have an abortion...I was very afraid...and he needed to tell his parents. We held each other for hours and cried.

In the days ahead, I stopped attending church. The previous January I had been nominated First Youth of the Year at my church, so I had a good reputation there. But news travels fast and now everyone at church knew about my pregnancy. Everyone. I was so humiliated that I stopped going. I felt as though I had let everyone down. I felt that no one could love me; that I had done something so wrong and so horrible I couldn't go back to that church. So I pulled away from almost everyone.

Bill finally got up the courage to tell his parents, and I was scheduled to arrive right afterward. Talking to Bill's parents had to be one of the hardest things I ever had to do. Now that they knew about the pregnancy, I didn't want to make eye contact with them. We sat at the kitchen table, all four of us, with Bill across from me, and we had a long talk. Thankfully, Bill's dad never raised his voice once at me, and they spoke very calmly. Bill's mom asked me if we would get married. I said that I loved Bill very much, but I wasn't ready to get married.

Bill's dad looked at me, and then at Bill, and said to him, "Do you hear what she said? She said she loves you."

Bill nodded and said, "Yeah…"

"Do you love her?"

My heart wanted to fall out of my chest because he just looked at me and didn't have an immediate response.

For a minute, there was silence, and Bill finally faced his dad and said, "Of course, I do."

Bill's dad quickly responded, "That's not what you told me earlier. You said that you really *care* about her. That's different than love. Do you *love* her?"

My mouth fell open, and I held my breath. Without looking at me, he finally said, "Yes, I love her."

I wasn't sure if I believed him. I asked to be excused and went to the bathroom. I cried and splashed water on my face. I realized that if I was going to fight to keep the baby, I would be fighting all alone. Composing myself, I went back into the kitchen.

Bill's dad wanted me to have an abortion. He only said it once. He wasn't forceful, and he wasn't mean. He just said, "If you want my opinion, I think you should have an abortion."

He made it clear that Bill would graduate from high school, and I said so would I. I had worked hard the first two years and my grades were pretty decent until this year. Lately I was losing ground in my classes, and I got a few Cs on my report card. But all in all, I really enjoyed high school.

I left Bill's house feeling more alone than ever. For the next eight weeks, I fought a losing battle with my mother. She became more and more angry. Every day, when I came home from school, she screamed at the top of her lungs about inconsequential things I did. Sometimes in our arguments, she slapped my face and called me a whore. I was so broken and so hurt, and I felt so abandoned.

Grandma's illness had gotten worse, and she had to be put into a nursing home so now I didn't have anyone to turn to. I laid awake at night trying to figure out how I could make it through all of this. Who could help? One day after coming home from school, I thought about finding my father. There had to be some way I could do it. I was 16 years old, but I had never seen him. I thought maybe if I found him, he could help me. Maybe he would stand beside me and help me fight my mom. I fell asleep with that one ray of hope in my thoughts.

The next day my mother was already angry when I got home from school. She screamed at me that I needed to have the abortion because if I didn't do it soon, it was going to be too late.

I took a new tactic and said, "You know, you need a parent's approval to have an abortion."

She frowned and said, "I'm your parent. What are you talking about?"

"Yeah, you're my mother, but you're not my father."

Her eyes grew so big, and she clenched her fists and ground her teeth together. She repeated, "What are you talking about?"

"Well, my father should have to sign for me to have an abortion, too."

She began to rage that she had custody of me and had every parental right to sign those papers without his consent. She stared hard at me for a minute and asked, "Do you really think he'd stop you from having an abortion? When I told him I was pregnant with you, he was so angry that he wanted me to have an abortion. When I refused, he packed his stuff and left. So if you think your father is going to save you, you're wrong." She stomped out and slammed the door behind her. I stood motionless and felt totally without hope. I wanted to die.

Trying to Solve the Problem

That night, as usual, I took care of my brother and two sisters while my mother was at work. I made them dinner and helped them a little bit with their homework. After I put them all to bed, I wrote a letter in my notebook to Bill telling him I loved him and that I was so sorry I had caused all this mess and had hurt his parents. I was especially sorry because I hurt the one person who was always so sweet to me. I told him I would solve the problem and make it go away.

After the kids were asleep, I got down the large bottle of vodka that my mom kept on top of the refrigerator and gulped enough to get myself drunk. I took a steak knife, stumbled into the bathroom, and locked the door. I sat down on the floor just like I had done when I was a little girl after bouts with my stepfather. I grasped the knife with my right hand and slit my wrist. I put the knife on the floor and my wrist over the toilet so that there wouldn't be any mess for anyone to clean up.

I passed out and finally awoke when my sister began knocking on the door because she had to use the bathroom. I sat up and my wrist hurt. I must have fallen down on the floor when I had lost consciousness. I looked at my wrist, and it was still bleeding a little. The toilet was full of blood and there was blood on the floor. I remember sitting there in amazement because I couldn't believe I was still alive. I yelled to my sister that I had fallen asleep in the bathtub and that I'd be out in just a few minutes.

I wrapped my wrist with toilet paper to stop the bleeding and covered it with a black bandanna. I quickly cleaned up the tiles and flushed all the paper down the toilet. Still feeling weak, I went to bed with my clothes on and drifted off into a heavy sleep.

The next day, I met Bill at school. He held me, and we left. We spent all day together talking and trying to hold each other up. One of the last questions he asked me was, "Are you sure we're doing the right thing?" I couldn't believe my ears. I felt that he had deserted me too. No one was on my side. No one but me wanted this child. I didn't know if I could keep on fighting for it.

CHAPTER FOURTEEN

The Decision

Each day, I reluctantly went home from school, dreading another confrontation with my mother. One afternoon, she started in on me again before I even had a chance to put my books down. She wanted to know what my decision was. I finally cracked. I couldn't handle it any more. I shouted at her, "Yes, I'll have the abortion if you'll just leave me alone! I'll have the abortion, but you're going to have to pay for it because I don't have the money and neither does Bill. Just stop yelling at me."

I threw my books down and escaped to the sink

where I vigorously began washing the dishes even though my wrist burned from the soap. My mother walked into the kitchen, put her hands on my shoulders, and hugged me. My body stiffened at her touch. I could hardly believe her sudden show of affection. She began to cry and said, "I'm doing this because I love you." Swiftly flicking away her tears, she left for work.

I looked after her and said, "Right."

My Last Chance

The abortion was scheduled for several days later. I thought for sure that I had killed the baby already because I had so much alcohol and bled so much. I thought maybe I wouldn't have to have an abortion because the baby was already dead. But I was wrong. Two days before the abortion, I hadn't started bleeding yet, so I realized that the baby hadn't died. My next thought was to run away. It was my last chance, my last hope. I packed another brown, paper bag with some clothes. I waited for my mom to go to sleep, and then snuck downstairs and took $20 out of my brother's wallet. I quietly let myself out the front door, carrying the brown paper bag.

I started walking down the dark, quiet street wondering where I could go. I decided to head for a nearby park where I could try and come up with a plan. *Where could I go?* The first idea that popped into my head was to try to find my dad. I didn't even know where to begin. Years ago when I had talked to my uncle, he had no idea where my father was. So that was out. I had no car and only the $20 I had taken from my brother. That wouldn't get me very far. I thought about going to Larry's house, but I knew that they'd find me there. I thought about going to one of my friends' houses, but they'd look for me there too. I guess I was looking for the edge of the earth so I could jump off. But when you're in so much pain and so much trouble, there is no place like that. This was reality, and I was at a loss as to what to do.

I sat on that swing in the middle of the night and cried. I started to think about my brother and my two sisters at home. Who would take care of them? Grandma was gone; my mom worked. My older brother built garages with my cousin for a living. There was nobody. What would happen to them?

You can't imagine how afraid I was. My mother had already made the appointment at the clinic. I tried to get out of it once when she told me the date of the abortion. I told her it was the last day of school, but she said she didn't care; the date was set. That was the earliest they could get me in, and that's when I was going.

I said to her, "Mom, are you sure? I just don't know. I don't know if this is right. Mom, it's a baby.

It's a little baby. How can they kill a baby?"

She said, "It's not a baby. It's not a baby yet. It looks like snot." She had watched somebody have an abortion once, and to her, it looked like a pile of snot.

There was no convincing her to change her mind. My mom was still so angry about it all. She told my sister that she wanted to put me in the car and get in an accident so I'd lose the baby. The only thing that was stopping her from carrying through with that plan was that the car wasn't paid off.

I was really afraid. I was afraid for my life. I wanted my mom to put her arms around me, to hold me, to support me, and to tell me it was going to be okay. I guess the fact was that it wasn't going to be okay. I couldn't understand why she wouldn't. I had helped her with the kids and the housework. It made perfect sense to me that she would help me. Now that Grandma was gone, I knew she had to work. For quite awhile now, I came home after school and willingly ironed her uniform, cleaned the house, did the laundry, and made dinner for the kids. It wasn't easy, and I didn't always do a great job, but I was only 16. I was still a kid myself. I couldn't understand what stopped her from helping me now when I needed her.

I finally decided to go back home because I had no other choice. I reluctantly left the park, took my brown paper bag and quietly snuck back into the house. I put the $20 back into my brother's wallet and went upstairs to bed.

The Day Arrived

On the day of the abortion, I was still trying to figure a way out of this mess. I thought to myself, *If anybody asks me if I'm sure about having the abortion, I'll cry or break down and share my feelings. Somebody's going to ask me. I know I'm going to see the counselor one more time before I do this.* I was sure of it.

We arrived early in the morning. I couldn't believe how many people were already in the waiting room. Mom wouldn't let Bill go with me; I had to go alone, with her.

They did a urine test, took my blood pressure, and listened to my heart and pulse. I kept waiting for someone to ask me if I was sure about what I was doing. They had a record of the last session when my mom blew up at the counselor. Didn't somebody see that I originally said I wanted to keep this baby, and now, here I was waiting to have an abortion? I kept waiting for somebody to ask me this question. I was hoping with everything in my heart for it to happen. I didn't dare pray because I knew I had let God down, too. But nobody spoke directly to me. My name was called, and I was taken back into a room with a table that had a bunch of equipment I had never seen before. I had never even had a pelvic exam or pap smear. The nurse told me to get undressed from the waist down, put on the paper gown, and sit on the table.

The doctor walked in and didn't even look at me or say hello. He put gloves on and read the chart. He sat down on his stool and got his tools out. He told the nurse to have me scoot down and put my feet in the stirrups. When he put a silver appliance inside me and opened me, I felt as if I was dying, I was in such pain. Then he put his hand completely inside me, and I felt as though I was being raped. I started to jerk away, and the doctor yelled at the nurse to hold me still. He pushed on my stomach, and I yelled out in pain. He wouldn't stop. He took a white 2-inch peg of some sort with something like a nailhead on it and went back inside me again. I tried to pull away, but the nurse held me down. The doctor snapped at the nurse, and she snapped at me. I grabbed the sides of the table, and I was shaking. He pulled away, unscrewed the appliance, and pulled it out. He snapped his gloves off and muttered "Done" and walked out the door.

I laid there feeling as humiliated as I did after a sexual abuse encounter. I felt as if I had just been brutally raped. The nurse sat me up and I was crying deep from my stomach. She looked at me and said, "We'll see you in a few hours."

I guessed later that the peg that was now inside me had to loosen my cervix so that they could put long silver staffs inside me for the suction part of the abortion. I put my clothes back on and rejoined my mother. It would take a few hours to work, so we went to have some lunch while we waited.

We went down the street to a restaurant, and I remember that my mom and I both had a crab salad croissant. I had about three bites before I started having contractions. I felt sick, ran to the bathroom, and started vomiting. I was in such pain. I couldn't eat, and I was crying and trying to hold myself together as best I could because I had to go back and sit with my mother. I finally managed to make it back out to the table, and soon we went back to the Planned Parenthood office. Other girls were starting to come back, too. It was getting late, and my mother had to be at work at 4:00. She went up to the lady at the desk and asked, "Can't we get this done? I can't be late for work."

The lady replied, "Well, the cervix has to be dilated a certain amount before they can do the actual abortion or else it could really hurt her." But they were going to try to move me up the list a little in order to get me out as soon as possible.

That was the beginning of the end. I realized there was no turning back; that the abortion was going to happen no matter what. Nobody had asked me if I was sure I wanted to go through with it, and I didn't have the courage to speak up. My name was called, and I was taken back into the same room. I had to get undressed and sit back on the table with my feet in the stirrups.

The doctor opened me up again, and I tried to hold still as he reached deep inside of me and pulled out the peg. Then he turned on a loud machine with a long, thin silver rod. The second he put it inside me, I screamed from my deepest being. It felt worse than any rape or abuse I had ever had to endure. I tried to jump off the table, but the doctor yelled at the nurse to hold me down and push me closer. Finally, I did the only thing that I knew how to do as a survivor—I looked up into the bright light, and I focused on it. I disconnected from my body, and it was over.

The next thing I knew, the machine was turned off and the loud roaring that sounded like a vacuum cleaner was gone. The doctor left without giving me a second look, and the nurse told me to get dressed. I remember pain traveling through my whole body as I tried to move. I sat on the chair doubled over, holding my stomach and rocking back and forth, back and forth, wanting so much to die. But I couldn't die.

Before my mom could come in, I ran to the bathroom, shut the door behind me, and locked it. I vomited until finally there was nothing left. I felt more hollow and more hopeless than *I had ever felt in my entire life*. I knew that I must have been in the bathroom awhile because they came and knocked on the door and asked me to come out. I told them I'd be out in just a minute, so I pulled myself up, splashed cold water all over my face, and ran my fingers through my long hair. I looked up, and in front of me was my reflection. I looked at myself in the mirror and saw that I was full of hatred and anger. I was in pain and blamed it all on myself. I hated the person I saw standing there in the mirror. I looked her straight in the eye with my teeth tightly clenched together and said, "I hate you. I hate you. I hate every part of you, and I will never, ever forgive you for what you just did."

That horrible experience was behind all of my self-hatred. I replayed those scenes over and over in my mind. I finally had gotten to the bottom of the last piece of emptiness in my life.

Through all my abuse, I felt as though I had God to turn to, but now I didn't feel that I could. Now I guessed I was truly alone. I didn't pray for forgiveness because I thought I had done something so wrong that God couldn't forgive me.

CHAPTER FIFTEEN

The Aftermath

After the abortion, I felt empty and hollow and certainly more violated than ever. A sadness that I had never felt before was ever present. I spent the entire summer despondent. I cried and often asked Bill to hold me. I would put his hand on my stomach and tell him that it hurt. It did still hurt. There was such an emptiness and such a deep regret.

The sadness didn't last, however, because it eventually turned into anger against myself. I was angry with myself that I hadn't fought harder...that I didn't speak up when I needed to speak up...that I didn't run away...that I didn't have the guts to take a chance and run no matter what the consequences were. I was even angry that I didn't have the guts to cut my wrists deep enough to die.

I used to look in the mirror when I was getting dressed and think, "I hate her." I would call myself names: *fat* and *ugly* and *whore* and *worthless*. The more I stared into the mirror and called myself those names, the more I began to believe them. I was angry with myself and swore I would never forgive myself so the pain would be with me for the rest of my life.

I was also angry with my mother. I didn't understand why she wouldn't help me. I didn't understand why she wouldn't support me when Grandma entered the nursing home. I was willing to help my mother because I knew she needed it. She was my mother, and I loved her. I would have done anything to help her. I couldn't understand why she wouldn't give me the help I so desperately needed.

That anger caused a break in my relationship with my mother. When she left the house she often said, "Remember, I'm not running no whorehouse."

I'd challenge her, "You know, you just called me a whore."

"No, I didn't. I said I'm not running a whorehouse."

"You know, it's the same thing."

"No, it's not."

But I believed that she thought I was a whore.

Path to Self-Destruction

After the abortion, I was on a path of self-destruction. By my senior year, I had cut my wrists four more times. I did it to let some of the pain out rather than to actually kill myself. There was so much pain, anger, and sorrow inside me, and I felt so alone. I felt abandoned and betrayed by my mother. Now my grandmother wasn't there either to help me or to protect me. I felt as if I were going to explode, so I ran a knife across my wrist just deep enough to cut through the first few layers of skin to let some blood come out. In some strange way, it felt like it released some of the pain.

When you leave marks on your body, they're hard to hide. The bandannas that I used to cover my marks were becoming "uncool" to wear at school, so I stopped the "cutting" and instead used food and alcohol to ease the pain. I drank as often as I could when no one was looking. I hid my alcoholism from everyone—Bill, my mother, and my friends. I crammed food down my throat in the middle of the night to try to fill the hollow feeling within me. Nothing seemed to work.

Bill was still with me. He seemed to be more in love with me than ever before. He held me, said that he loved me, and told me that I was beautiful. He told me all the nice and wonderful things that girls want to hear, but I didn't believe him. I began setting myself up for pain because I believed that's all I deserved—not the happiness or joy that a normal person expects. I hated myself from the inside out. For the life of me, I couldn't understand how Bill could still care about me. So slowly, I began pushing him away, a little farther and a little farther until one day, I pushed him so far away that he wouldn't come back. I tried to make up with him. I tried to tell him I was sorry, but he didn't buy it. I had hurt him too badly. So that was that. I was left alone in my pain, just like I wanted to be.

Through all my abuse and sexual assaults, I felt as though I had God to turn to, but now I didn't feel that I could. That was hard to bear; now I guessed I was truly alone. I didn't pray any prayers of forgiveness because I thought I had done something so wrong that God couldn't forgive me. I believed in my heart I had committed murder, and I didn't think I could be forgiven. The only thing I could pray for was to die. Sometimes the pain is so great in your life that death seems to be the only answer, the only way to stop the pain.

I tried to put on a facade and live the life of a normal teenager going to the prom. My senior year, I knew I was running out of time. It was November, so

I knew I didn't have much time to plan my future. I was becoming an adult, and I needed to have some kind of plan for my life. I applied at some colleges and took my SAT tests, but I didn't have any hope. I tried to put on a front that everything was okay. But I didn't feel like I fit in anywhere—at school or at home—and I felt unloved. I couldn't go back to church because I had let everybody down. I was humiliated, and I couldn't face them.

I think that self-destruction became my plan. I had gotten a job the summer before my senior year, and that made me very dangerous because now I had my own money, and money presents opportunity. Alcohol was easy to buy because I always looked older than my age. I walked into a grocery store, bought peach schnapps, wine coolers, and some potato chips. I threw in some normal household items such as a loaf of bread, some lunchmeat, and maybe some nylons and toothpaste to make it look more like "legitimate" purchases. I turned a friend's class ring around so it looked like a wedding band. When I stood in the checkout line, I chatted with whoever was in front of me and with the girl who was running the cash register. The topic of conversation always came around to husbands, and I'd make comments about socks left on the floor all the time. We'd have a conversation about my "husband" that I made up. She bagged all the groceries, and I paid her with my check. So I got all the alcohol that I wanted. I spent my senior year slowly drinking myself into oblivion.

Vodka was the best thing to drink because it had no odor. I drank it before and after school and before and after work. I drank socially with my friends so that nobody really knew how much I drank. I became very careless when it came to sex. I started dating different people, putting myself and even some of my friends in dangerous situations. Once I went out with a student from Purdue University, who was in his early 20s. We went to a steakhouse down the street, had a few drinks, and something to eat. He invited me to go to Chicago with some of his other friends, so I asked him if I could bring a girlfriend along. I asked Jennifer to come with me. After picking us up, they drove to a house where there was a group of 20-year-olds on cocaine. I was so shocked that he snorted cocaine right in front of me that I told him I wanted to leave.

I said, "You know, I don't want to date someone who needs to get loaded before they go out with me." I made him take me home. The statement was funny when you realize that I had downed five glasses of vodka before we left for the party. I guess I didn't count that as a drug. I was feeding myself a lie.

Things at home were extremely bad. My mother and I grew farther and farther apart all the time. It was very difficult to carry on a conversation with her. I felt that she was still angry and furious with me because I'd gotten pregnant. One of the hardest times was when my older brother thought he might have gotten his girlfriend pregnant. We sat at the kitchen table, and my brother cried because he was very afraid. His girlfriend's dad was a very angry man who didn't care for my brother and didn't like his daughter going out with him.

My mom looked at my brother and said, "If she's pregnant and her father kicks her out, she can come and live here."

My jaw dropped open, and I just stared at her.

She turned to me defensively and asked, "What?"

I said, "I cannot believe you!"

I ran up the stairs crying. I felt so betrayed that my mother was willing to take in another girl off the street—my brother's girlfriend—and would help her raise their baby, but she wouldn't help her own daughter.

My mother became more and more controlling, and I wanted nothing more than to break out. It looked as though Prince Charming wasn't coming to rescue me, so I needed to do something. I didn't know what. I didn't know how to handle my life. I was being eaten alive by the pain from inside out, and I felt hollow and abandoned and betrayed. I couldn't stand to look at myself in the mirror. I didn't want to be alive. I prayed to die. I didn't believe in a future.

Living for Tomorrow

And then I met Joe. There was so much laughter inside him—maybe enough for the two of us. And he had hope. He had hope for the future. He wanted to graduate. He couldn't wait to get a job and start living life. He had plans. He had goals, and he wrote his goals out on paper. I'd never met anyone like him before. He was amazing to me. He laughed all the time. And I knew that he was going to save me.

So I started living for tomorrow. I didn't know how to live in today yet. I got up and dressed. I did the mechanical things that you need to do. By the second semester of my senior year, I only went to school half days because I already had all the credits I needed to graduate. I stayed for social reasons and because I was working on my high school newspaper. At first, I was a reporter and then front-page editor. It was the only thing I really enjoyed doing. I was responsible for a couple of pages in the senior yearbook and was inducted into Quill and Scroll. That year, I won an award for being the most valuable staffer. I was nominated for the *Hammond Times* Award and for the *Calumet Press* Award. It gave me something to focus on until tomorrow came. And that's all I talked about. I talked about tomorrow because tomorrow had hope. Joe and I were planning to get married. We were planning a future. We were planning a life. I believed that he had enough hope for tomorrow for both of us. So that's what I did. I started to live for tomorrow and just survive today.

Looking back at the last few years, Joe is one of the main reasons why I made it this far through recovery. He helped me face some of the difficult events of my past. But the abortion was one thing I would have to face on my own. At least I finally knew what was plaguing me, why I was still hurting myself with food. Joe couldn't begin to fathom the issues that a woman goes through after an abortion, and so I learned to lean on God in a new way at this stage of my recovery.

*I chose to forgive my mother,
to forgive myself, and to let go of the pain.
I looked at the past, and saw it for
what it was, forgave those who let me
down, and for the first time experienced
a release from all the pain!*

CHAPTER SIXTEEN

The Final Resolution

When I began to sort things out at this point, I clearly saw there were two areas that needed resolving. The first one was my relationship with my mom. That 16-year-old girl would never have had an abortion if she had not been pressured into making the decision by her mother.

I went to my pen and paper once again, and I wrote as if it were yesterday when I was still 16, and the abortion was performed. I remembered all the hideous arguments between my mom and me. I allowed that 16-year-old girl to write letters to her mother saying all the things she had never had the courage to say. Over and over again in these letters, the word *hate* came across the page. "I hate you. I hate you for what you did to me. I hate you for forcing me into this abortion. I hate everything about you. I hated that you were my mother." There was so much anger on these pages. It went from hate to resentment. "I resented helping you. I resented that I had to watch your children. I resented that I ironed your uniform. I resented that I had to do your laundry, and I resented that I had to clean your house."

After I had gotten all of this out, what started to come across the pages wasn't hate and resentment anymore. "You let me down. I needed you and I wanted you to be there for me. I needed you to hold me and protect me. You let me down. I felt abandoned by you. I know that you were there physically, but I needed you to support me emotionally. I needed you to wrap your arms around me and tell me it was going to be okay. I needed you to tell me that you loved me." That's what came across the last few pages from the 16-year-old girl who was hurt and wounded. It became apparent that behind all the anger, hatred, and resentment was a sense of abandonment.

I went on to the next step. I began to peel away the layers of pain like you might peel the layers of an onion. Next I wrote as the young woman in her mid-twenties with three children who had not yet experienced any recovery.

Again when I addressed my mother, the first thing that came across the pages was hatred: "I hate you. You're not there for me. I need you to be my friend. I need to lean on you. We have no relationship, and I resent what you did to me." There were only a couple of pages of resentment. What followed was: "Why can't you love me? Why can't you reach out and hold me and put your arms around me and kiss my cheek the way you do with your grandchildren? Why? Am I so different from them? Am I not as precious to you as those grandchildren are to you?"

People told me that my mother was trying to love me through my children. I wrote to her: "That's a lie. I'm right here, and if you want to love me, *love* me. Don't love me through my kids. Love *me*. I'm still your daughter. Treat me the way you treat them. It hurts me to watch you tell your grandchildren that you love them two or three times in one visit when, as a 25-year-old woman, the last time I remember hearing those words from you was on my wedding day many years before. I feel abandoned by you."

Finally I let myself speak as the 31-year-old woman who had some healing behind her. I decided to talk about the *facts* of the situation instead of the *feelings*.

There were a number of facts that I had never faced until now. Fact: At the time of the abortion, my mother was 38 years old and was divorced twice. Her second husband was in prison. She had five children to support, aged 8-18. That's a lot of responsibility even for a man and a woman who are happily married, building their relationship, and earning two incomes. My mother worked two jobs as a waitress to try to make ends meet. She worked long, hard hours. She was tired. She was in a relationship with a man who was extremely violent and verbally abusive. I decided my mother was probably depressed herself.

Another fact: When I had gotten pregnant, my grandmother was very sick and went into the hospital, where they found water on her brain. My mother lived with her five children in my grandmother's house, and we had nowhere else to go. They were afraid when my grandmother came out of surgery that she would have to enter a nursing home and wouldn't be able to come home. So my mom tried to work things out so that Medicaid wouldn't take the house, which was the only thing my grandmother really owned. The family made arrangements to put the house in my mom's name, but found out it should have been done four years before my grandmother went into the nursing home. The lawyers told my mother and my aunts that there was a good chance the house would be taken from my mother.

Another fact: My mother saw me as a 16-year-old girl with a lot of opportunity. I did fairly well in high school. I wasn't a scholar, but I did well and enjoyed school. I had every intention of going to college until I became pregnant. My mother saw those dreams for her 16-year-old daughter fly right out the window. She knew the lifestyle I was choosing. From experience, she knew the ramifications of raising a child alone without any help from the father. She wanted a better life for me than what she had.

So the facts were that not only did my mother have five children she was trying to raise herself; her mother was sick; she didn't know where we were going to live; and then her 16-year-old daughter became pregnant.

As a 31-year-old woman, I saw that in fact my mother *did* love me. She was trying to provide me with an option, an option to live a life that she missed. She tried to solve my problem with a solution that was different from what she chose when she was young with an unplanned pregnancy. I believe the facts show she was trying to do the best thing for me.

Now, facts *do not justify* any behavior, not by any means. However, facts *make the behavior understandable*. There's a difference between feelings and facts. As a 16-year-old child, I believed my mother didn't love me. Those were my feelings. But the facts show that, indeed, she did love me. So now, it was my turn. It was my turn as a 31-year-old woman who's walked a recovery path, who's felt healing and joy in her life, to sit down and write a letter to her mom. The letter to my mom was short, and my feelings were all laid aside. This 31-year-old woman wrote the following letter to her mother.

Dear Mom,
I do not agree with your decision for the abortion. However, today for the first time in my life, I understand your reasons. Today, I choose to let go of this pain. Today, I choose to forgive you.

Forgiving Myself

The issue with my mother was settled once and for all. But that was only half of it. There were two parts to my pain. The first was my mom, but the second was myself. I still had a difficult time looking at myself in the mirror even after all these years of recovery. I continued to hurt myself with food because I didn't value myself. I looked at myself and believed I was worth nothing. And the reason why? I was full of a lot of *should haves* in connection with the abortion. I "should have" run away. That's what I would say to myself as I looked in the mirror and saw that 16-year-old kid. I hated her, and I was angry with her. I'd say, *You should have run away. You should have fought harder. What is the matter with you? Why did you quit? You should have said no. You should have kept saying no over and over again until somebody finally heard you. You should have protected your own child. What is the matter with you? The child couldn't protect itself. It was your job. You should have protected your own child.*

And then my mind raced to the scene in that abortion clinic. *You should have made a scene. You sat there waiting for someone to say something to you. You should have said, "Wait, I'm not sure." You should have. But you didn't. You should have saved that child's life, and you are responsible for that child's death.*

I spent many, many years abusing myself in front of a mirror with those very words. Now, it was time to stand in front of that mirror and let it go. So I walked in front of my mirror with the door shut and locked. I lit a candle because I don't think I really wanted to see my reflection clearly. But it was time that we met face to face. I looked at that reflection and talked to that 16-year-old girl, saying, *You were scared. That's why you didn't run away. I understand that. Today, I understand that you didn't know what to do, that you were trying to crawl away inside, and you didn't feel that there was anyone around you to protect you. Today, I understand that you fought as hard as you could. Today, I believe that you tried to stand up to every confrontation that you could until every ounce of your body just gave in; until the fear overtook you. Today, I believe that you fought until you couldn't fight anymore. Today, I believe that you did the best you could with what you had at the time. You didn't have the skills that you needed to be able to fight the fight.*

Today, I know that you're sorry with every thread of your being. If you could go back and change the past, you would. But you can't. Today, I understand that. I believe that God forgives you. I know that you've crawled upon your knees in the darkest hours and cried thousands of tears, begging for forgiveness. I'm telling you that God forgives you. And most importantly, today, I'm telling you that I'm choosing to forgive you, too.

I chose to forgive my mother, to forgive myself, and to let go of the pain. I looked at the past, and saw it for what it was, forgave those who let me down, and for the first time experienced a release from all the pain!

CHAPTER SEVENTEEN

Giving Her to God

The next step I took was to spend some time alone with God. I wanted to know the best way to take the final step in my recovery and give all of this—especially everything surrounding the abortion—to Him. Friends in my recovery talked about having a funeral for the baby. At the time, my sorrow was too great, and I still had too much to work through. But today, I chose to be ready. I decided to have a funeral for my aborted child.

The first thing I did was give my child a name. I believe with all my heart that the baby was a girl. I feel certain about this because from the very beginning, I knew what each one of my children was going to be. I believed that this baby was a girl, so I named her Sara Angel.

The second thing I needed for the funeral was a coffin. I took a shoebox and emptied it to use at the burial. I bought Sara a tiny, white dress full of lace around the collar and the bottom. It was decorated all over with tiny orchid flowers. I bought a white, lacy bonnet and little white shoes. I found a receiving blanket with angels that had little splashes of orchids on their gowns. I opened the receiving blanket and laid the white dress in it and put it in the box. I laid her little shoes at one end and her little bonnet at the other. I wrote a birth certificate and drew little orchids around the sides of it. I wrote the words, "To this child, I give the name Sara Angel" and signed it "Mother of this child, Kelly Daniel Vates." I placed it on top and closed the lid. I took the box and my Bible out to a special place and sat down on the ground.

I read Psalm 139:13-16.

For You created my innermost being. You knit me together in my mother's womb. I praise You because I am fearfully and wonderfully made. Your works are wonderful, I know that full well. My frame was not

*hidden from You when I was laid in the se-
cret place. When I was woven together in the
depths of the earth, Your eyes saw my un-
formed body. All the days ordained for me
were written in Your book before one of them
came to be.*

All those years, I believed that if I kept Sara alive
in my head, I wouldn't forget her death. In her
honor, I tortured myself with the memories of the
abortion every day. But now I knew that was futile.
Today, I chose to ask God to take this pain from my
heart, and I chose to completely let her go and leave
her in the hands of God. I dug a hole just large
enough for the small shoebox and put the box in it. I
pulled out a letter that I wrote to Sara, which read,

Dear Sara Angel,
There are so many things I want to say to
you. First, I will start by saying that I love
you very much. There has not been a day
that has passed in my life that I have not
thought of you. And I've carried you with me
in my mind. I believed by never letting you
go, I was somehow keeping you alive. Today, I
am choosing to turn you over to your heavenly Father. I pray that you will find the same
unconditional love and peace in His arms

that I have found. Today, I am asking for your forgiveness. I know I let you down, and I am very sorry. Today, I am choosing to let go of the pain of your death. Today, I am choosing a life full of joy, full of peace, full of love, and full of happiness. And I choose to do this in honor of you. I will always be your mother, and I will always love you.

I took the letter and set it on fire. After all the ashes had cooled, I picked them up, put them in the box, and closed the lid. As tears streamed down my face, I softly covered the box with handful after handful of dirt.

Many thoughts and feelings went through my heart and mind. Some of them were old ones such as, *How can you forgive yourself for this? How can you let go of this pain? You're walking away from her again.* These lasted for only a moment or two. With God's help and grace, the healthy, healing side of me began saying that torturing myself with thoughts of her death day by day was not keeping her alive. The only thing it was doing was eating me from the inside out. The only way to truly show Sara that I loved her very much was by turning her completely over to God and letting go. My heart ached as I sat by that tree with the warm sun and soft breezes. I played some special music I had brought with me. Finally I put my hand on top of the loose dirt and asked God to take Sara and all the pain, and to forgive and heal me. After a few quiet minutes, I pulled myself up, gathered my things, and slowly walked away. Part of me wanted to turn around. I stopped after a few steps. Sometimes letting go of familiar pain is scary. At least in the familiar pain, you know what to expect. *Who am I going to be without all the pain any more?* So the choice was mine. *Do I hold onto the pain of yesterday or do I walk toward the promise of tomorrow?*

I looked back one more time, cried a little more, and then I softly said goodbye. I turned and began to walk toward tomorrow.

Life today is wonderful. I look back at where I've been and feel so grateful for where I am today. The process of recovery is just that—a process. Each day I continue to grow a little more, learn something new, and hear something inspiring.

EPILOGUE

Today, I choose to live each moment of each day. I choose to value myself with my words, my mind, and my actions. I choose to set myself free from the prison of yesterday. Today, I am healed and live a life of joy.

Living a life of joy is like constantly being hugged from the inside out. That's how life is supposed to be. No more trying to "stuff" my pain with food or any other novocaine. The pain has been healed, and the healing has left joy—the kind of joy where you feel a warmth when you smile or laugh.

Now I look in the mirror and no longer see an image of yesterday. I have learned how to love and nurture myself. I used to stand in front of a mirror and see the prison I had locked myself up in. I had allowed my body to get large so that no one would be able to get close to me. I began breaking down this physical prison. Today, I take 20-30 minutes each morning to exercise. I ride my stationary bike when my children are at school and my husband is at work. I turn the music up very loud, pedal my bike, and sing along with the music. I do this each morning not because I love to exercise. I do it because I AM WORTH IT. To participate in the life I have been blessed with, I have to get in shape. This is the only body I get. Like it or not, it's my responsibility to take care of it.

Nurturing yourself is so much fun. I have learned to love it. There are simple things I enjoy such as reading a good book, taking a long bubblebath, painting my fingernails, or getting a haircut. I have had my eyebrows and facial hair waxed—what a boost to my self-confidence. I love the way it makes me feel. Styling my hair, wearing make up, treating myself to a facial, wearing clothes that make me feel good about myself—these are practical things I do to care for myself.

Taking walks in the park on a warm day... swinging on a swing or sitting on a park bench in the sunshine...having lunch with a friend...these are more of the little things that bring me so much enjoyment. I even make yearly doctor's appointments (and keep them), have my teeth cleaned, and my eyes checked. These might sound like mundane things that everyone takes for granted. But for me, these are positive actions that I take to rebuild my life.

I spent many years of my life calling myself names. These words were my way of continuing to abuse myself and tear myself down. Today, I use words to build myself up. I stand in front of the mirror and smile. I say: "I look nice today. I love my hair, this color looks nice on me." I journal positive words: "I am a valuable person; I am special; I am creative; I am beautiful. I have a great personality; I am funny; and I love being me." Words are very powerful in my life, especially now that I've learned to use them in a positive way.

The Mind

My mind is still the most challenging battlefield for me. I can say nice things to myself in a mirror, but it is so much harder to accept them when I hear other people say them to me. My first reaction is, *Oh, please!* A valuable person? *Give me a break.* My mind is a memory bank, and it has not forgotten the past. It has all the evidence it needs to prove that I am not what I say I am.

The mind is like a computer. It only processes what it has been given. In the past, my mind was manipulated into believing the lies of my abusers. No more! I have been reprogramming it as I continue to say positive affirmations to myself, write them in my journal, and accept them from others. My mind is beginning to believe the things I say about myself as truth. The old files are being written over by the new ones. It's a process, however, and one that takes time and dedication. However, I am worth it. Now when my husband says I am beautiful, I no longer roll my eyes and think he is just saying that because he has to. I hold my head high, smile, and say, "Thank you."

Living life today is wonderful. I look back at where I've been and feel so grateful for where I am today. The process of recovery is just that—a process. It's one that continues. Each day I continue to grow a little more, learn something new, and hear something inspiring. The process of growth is never ending. I work at it every day. I spend time reading, watching, learning, and praying.

One of the most precious results from my recovery is the peace I now experience. The sleepless nights are gone, and I live in peace. The pain is healed. I can see myself as a valuable person today because I now see myself through the love of God. I wish I could share my peace with every survivor of childhood sexual abuse. I wish I could share my peace with every woman who struggles with the regret of an abortion. I wish I could share my peace with each child, man, and woman who has been beaten, abandoned, neglected, and made to feel worthless. I would share my peace to end their pain, but I can't. Each person has to find it for themselves.

Now when the storms of life rage against me, as they do from time to time for everyone, I close my eyes, take in a deep breath, and repeat the following words over and over. Slowly, the panic of today eases and peace once again fills my body, mind, and spirit. I hope they will help and comfort you as much as they do me:

The Lord is my shepherd, I shall lack nothing. He makes me lie down in green pastures; He leads me beside quiet waters. He restores my soul. He leads me down the path of righteousness for His name's sake. Even though I walk through the valley of the shadow of death, I will fear no evil, for you are with me; your rod and your staff, they comfort me. You prepare a table before me in the presence of my enemies. You anoint my head with oil; my cup overflows. Surely goodness and love will follow me all the days of my life, and I will dwell in the house of the Lord forever.
(Psalm 23)

Note to the reader: My counselor, Lynne, was the one I have shared everything with, but who still hugged me before I left her office. She validated my pain but never encouraged me to stay there. She cheered for me but never carried me. She always listened with her heart. She shares some insights below that were helpful to me and I hope will be to you, too.

APPENDIX

From the Counselor's Notebook

When children are sexually abused, the effect seems to reach to the core of who they are, affecting them in ways they may not realize until years later. The abuse seems to impact most, if not all, areas of their lives, depending upon the severity of the situation.

The degree of impact on children when they are sexually abused depends on a variety of factors: the closeness of the relationship to the abuser, the severity of the abuse, whether or not threats and/or physical abuse are combined with the sexual abuse, the age of the child, the duration of the abuse, whether or not the child is able to tell someone about the abuse, and whether they are believed and protected from further abuse. As the degree and number of the above factors involved in the abuse increases, so does the overall damage to the child. It is necessary for survivors to carefully and objectively assess each of these areas in order to understand how they are impacted in the present. Since most survivors remain very stuck in their childhood thinking patterns, it is often necessary for them to have an objective person to help with this process. A therapist, a close friend who is relatively emotionally healthy, a therapy or support group for survivors, or a pastor may be helpful.

Usually everything from self-esteem and self-confidence to healthy body image and relationships are damaged. These children usually experience shame and guilt over what was done to them because they attribute the responsibility to themselves. This is a natural reaction for children, who are, by nature and level of maturity, egocentric, seeing themselves as the center and cause of everything. Until children are in their early to mid teens, they are cognitively immature and thus unable to objectively evaluate what they are told but instead swallow it whole. Consequently, if children are told that they caused or wanted the sexual activity, they will usually believe what they are told. With that in mind, it is not difficult to understand how such adults will suffer low self-esteem, rooted in shame and guilt.

Closely associated with low self-esteem is re-
duced self-confidence. Many children who were
abused thought that they should have been able to
prevent or stop the abuse. This again results from
their egocentricity combined with their natural lack
of power as children. As they grow up, they experience a sense of powerlessness to navigate the world
and handle a variety of situations which arise in
their lives. As a consequence, they frequently assume a victim position in which they are powerless
to cope and to change. What they need to realize is
what I have heard so many survivors say, "I was just
a child!" It is necessary for them to return in their
minds to their state at the time of the abuse, and, for
the first time, realize that they were relatively powerless against an adult and that they did what they
had to do to survive.

Survivors of childhood sexual abuse also have
poor body images. This sometimes results from the
experience of having their bodies respond in some
way to the sexual stimulation to which they were exposed, which seems like a major betrayal by their
bodies, and additionally, gives credence to any sug-
gestion that they wanted or liked the sexual activity.
It is necessary for them to realize that children, as
well as adults, have sexual responses, and that they
are often unaware of them prior to being sexually
abused. How can one expect oneself to control some-

thing of which one is not even aware? As adults, these survivors may be fearful of sex as well as relationships in general. On the other hand, children who are praised for their physical attributes in the context of sexual abuse or who learn that by submitting to the sex, they can avoid worse abuse or earn favors, come to the conclusion that their bodies are objects to be used. This frequently leads to shallow relationships if not to some form of prostitution. Body image may be further implicated if survivors choose added weight as a protection from the sexual interest of others.

Relationships for survivors are frequently a difficult area. Poor self-esteem and lack of self-confidence often cause the survivor to choose relationships out of a tremendous need to be loved, which makes them very vulnerable to ignoring warning signs of an unhealthy, or even dangerous, relationship. The more severe the abuse factors, the more likely the survivor is to choose a mate who will be abusive in some way. If the survivor was abused by one or more trusted caregivers and/or if other caregivers refused to believe and protect them, trust in relationships becomes a huge issue. Since our concept of and relationship with God seems to derive early on from the way we are treated by our primary caregivers, it is not surprising that many survivors of abuse have a very fearful, negative concept of God. They tend to either see God as punitive and untrustworthy, and/or themselves as unworthy of His love and provision. This is an area which seems to be very difficult to heal and truly seems to require the "renewing of the mind" spoken of in Romans 12:2. Survivors of abuse have accepted a self-concept derived from an assumption that they are the center of the universe, that they are hopeless and unworthy of love because they are damaged goods. What is needed is for their concept of who they are to be rooted in who Christ is and what He has done for them and for us all.

Forgiveness tends to be a huge issue for most survivors, since they often think that forgiving their abusers and other caregivers means to excuse what they did. This couldn't be farther from the truth. It is even a contradiction in terms; if something is excusable, there would be no need for forgiveness. Survivors also frequently fail to realize that forgiveness is as much or more for their benefit than for that of the offender and is necessary for their complete healing. It is not surprising that the Bible repeatedly commands forgiveness. Sometimes survivors prefer the terms "making peace with" or "letting go of" instead of forgiveness. Whatever term is used, forgiveness by survivors is healing for them and frees them from the "stuckness" in their past abuse issues and enables them to continue to become who God created them to be. They are increasingly freed to be in healthy relationships with others, including God.

The good news is that Jesus died and rose again, so that everyone (yes, that includes survivors!) who believes in Him can not only have eternal life but may benefit from the healing that is available through His resurrection power. Isaiah 53:5 promises that "by His wounds we are healed." Those who choose to accept Jesus and offer Him their lives to heal and to use will find peace and healing they had not dreamed possible. And it's an exciting journey to see how He can redeem the rotten, stinking lemons of sexual abuse and turn them into refreshing lemonade in one's own life as well as in the lives of others (Romans 8:28).

—*Lynne B. Scherschel, LMFT*

Lynne Scherschel graduated from Purdue University with a degree in counseling and took two years post graduate training in Marriage and Family Therapy. She is a licensed marriage and family therapist and has been in practice for 15 years. She is a clinical member of the American Association of Marriage and Family Therapists and a member of the American Association of Christian Counselors.

A Note From Kelly...

Shattered Innocence was written in honor of and dedicated to all survivors of childhood sexual abuse. In recovery, when someone shares their story, it gives another survivor a voice. That is my intent, to give all survivors a chance to have a voice. Those are the founding principals for SEAS of Life Ministries (S.E.A.S.= Survivors Empowering All Survivors). Validation and support during your walk on the path of recovery is so important.

For my next project, I need to hear from you. What is the most difficult issue YOU deal with in recovery? What helps keep you grounded? How do you build a support system? How do you deal with flashbacks, body memories, and panic attacks? Share your struggles and your triumphs. Let me know what issues are most important to you on your path to wholeness.

You can visit our website at:

http://www.seasoflife.com

Or you can email us at

letters@seasoflife.com

Or write us at:

SEAS of Life Ministries

P.O. Box 1634

Highland, IN 46322

Thank you for reading and caring and sharing!

—*Kelly Vates*

OTHER RESOURCES FOR SURVIVORS

RAINN
The Rape, Abuse and Incest National Network
operates the national sexual assault hotline:
800-656-HOPE.
It will connect you automatically
to your local rape crisis center,
which can provide counseling and support.
More information is at their website:
www.rainn.org

SEXUAL ASSAULT RECOVERY PROJECT
Victim Assistance Unit
Porter County Prosecutors Office
16 E. Lincoln Way, Suite 527
Valpo, IN 46383
219-465-3408
Email: LRohrich@porterco.org

SURVIVORS OF INCEST ANONYMOUS
P.O. Box 190
Benson, MD 21018
410-893-3322
website: 222.siawso.org

OTHER BOOKS ON RECOVERY
PUBLISHED BY EVERGREEN PRESS

HIDDEN CASTLE
The story of one woman's struggle to be free from a seemingly hopeless addiction and her desperate search for the hidden key that would release her. Included are helpful insights for using the 12-step recovery programs.
ISBN 096373119X TPB 144 PG. $7.95

SEEDS OF THE HEART
A year's worth of daily devotions for those in recovery, helping them with inner healing. These meditations will strengthen the reader's love for God and themselves.
ISBN 0963731149 TPB 288 pg. $12.95

WHEN THE PETAL FALLS
A strong message of hope and healing for women who are struggling because of abuse. Practical advice and encouragement to become all that God meant you to be.
ISBN 1581690517 PB 160 pg. $9.95

INSPIRATIONAL BOOKS
TREASURED MOMENTS WITH GOD
Prophetic words of encouragement. Each message is a personal word of hope, help, and assurance in the midst of daily struggles. ISBN 1581690142 PB 136 pg. $7.99

THE POWER OF FORGIVENESS
True stories of exceptional forgiveness coupled with practical insights from the scriptures. Learn powerful keys to forgiveness that will change your life forever.
ISBN 1581690509 PB 96 pg. $5.95